DISEASES

3rd Revised Edition

Volume 2

Blood to Crohn's disease

Bryan Bunch
and
Jenny Tesar
EDITORS

GROLIER
an imprint of
SCHOLASTIC
Scholastic Library Publishing
www.scholastic.com/librarypublishing

Editors: Bryan Bunch and Jenny Tesar, Scientific Publishing

Design and production: G & H SOHO, Inc.
  Design: Gerry Burstein
  Prepress: Kathie Kounouklos

Writers:

Barbara Branca
Bryan Bunch
Barbara A. Darga
Betsy Feist
Gene R. Hawes
Wendy B. Murphy
Karin L. Rhines
Jenny Tesar
Bruce Wetterau
Gray Williams

Editorial assistant:
Marianne Bunch

Copyediting:
Felice Levy

Index
Felice Levy and Marianne Bunch

Creative assistance:
Pam Forde

Illustrators:

Photography supervisor:
Karin L. Rhines

Photographs:
Karin L. Rhines *(except where noted)*

Icons:
Steve Virkus and Karen Presser

Medical Illustrations:
Jean Cassels, Leslie Dunlap, Pamela Johnson, and Joel Snyder

Library of Congress Cataloging-in-Publication Data

Diseases / Bryan Bunch and Jenny Tesar, editors. — 3rd rev. ed.
      p. cm.
    Includes index.
    Summary: Alphabetically arranged articles presenting medical
  information on more than 500 diseases, discussing causes, symptoms,
  stages of the disease, its likelihood of striking, treatments, prevention,
  and long-term effects.
    ISBN 0-7172-6205-7 (set) — ISBN 0-7172-6206-5 (v. 1) — ISBN
  0-7172-6207-3 (v. 2) — ISBN 0-7172-6208-1 (v. 3) — ISBN 0-7172-6209-X
  (v. 4) — ISBN 0-7172-6210-3 (v. 5) — ISBN 0-7172-6211-1 (v. 6) — ISBN
  0-7172-6212-X (v. 7) — ISBN 0-7172-6213-8 (v. 8)   1. Diseases —
  Encyclopedias, Juvenile.   I. Bunch, Bryan H.   II. Tesar, Jenny E.

  R130.5.D57   2006
  616.003—dc22   2006007986

Third revised edition published 2006, by Scholastic Library Publishing.
First published in the United States in 1997 by
Grolier Educational, Sherman Turnpike, Danbury, CT 06816

Set ISBN-10: 0-7172-6205-7
Set ISBN-13: 978-0-7172-6205-2

Volume ISBN-10: 0-7172-6207-3
Volume ISBN-13: 978-0-7172-6207-6

Blood

On the Internet
KIDS HEALTH
kidshealth.org/parent/general/
body_basics/blood.html

Blood is a complex substance that contains several different kinds of cells suspended in a fluid that is filled with various proteins and other chemicals. The mix of water and chemicals that remains when cells are removed is a clear yellow liquid called *plasma* (PLAAZ-muh) or (when separated from proteins involved in clotting) *serum* (SIHR-uhm).

Location and amount: Blood is the body's only liquid organ. It is normally inside veins and arteries throughout the body, which together form the *bloodstream*. The smallest passages for blood, the capillaries, have such thin walls that parts of blood pass through them when needed; for example, disease-fighting cells can leave the bloodstream. But if a break in the bloodstream occurs, such as a cut or even a small tear in an artery, escaped whole blood can be dangerous to the cells nearby, largely because of the pressure it can exert on them.

The normal amount of blood in a human is about 10 to 12 pounds in a person weighing around 150 pounds. A man has more blood than a woman of the same weight. A 150-pound man has about 11 or 12 pints of blood, while a woman of that weight has only 8 or 9 pints, and a woman weighing less has even less, with 7 pints about the average.

Blood is constantly on the move. In 20 seconds a specific drop of blood can circulate completely from the heart, through the body, and back to the heart. That is because blood travels at an average rate of 0.7 miles per hour.

Role: Different parts of blood have different functions. The red color of blood comes from *erythrocytes* (ih-RIHTH-ruh-SIYTZ), commonly known as *red blood cells*. Erythrocytes lack nuclei and internal structure. They are produced by cells in the bone marrow (called *stem cells*) for just one purpose—to carry needed oxygen to cells and to remove carbon dioxide, which is produced when cells use the oxygen.

Marrow stem cells also make several varieties of *white blood cells*, such as lymphocytes and phagocytes, which are important parts of the immune system that fights bacteria, virusus, and other invaders.

Another component of blood made by marrow stem cells

Healthy persons are able to stay healthy with a somewhat smaller amount of blood than is normally in their circulatory system, and the body quickly replaces any lost. Many illnesses can be alleviated with whole blood or with parts of blood, such as plasma or antibodies, and accident victims often lose much of their blood supply, so donated blood has been a major factor in saving lives in the past century. Here students from Purdue University in Indiana donate blood in response to the 9/11 terrorist attacks on the United States in 2001. (Purdue News Service Photo by David Umberger)

is the *platelets*. These cell fragments play a critical role in forming blood clots, which stop blood from flowing out of the body if there is a break in the wall of a blood vessel.

Thousands of different proteins are dissolved in the blood plasma. The two major groups of blood proteins are albumin and globulin. Albumin helps carry medications and other substances through the blood, and maintains blood pressure. Globulins include antibodies that fight infection. Doctors can use the blood levels of certain proteins to look for health problems. For example, the presence of creatine-kinase MB, released by some dying heart cells, is used to diagnose heart attacks.

Conditions that affect the blood: Most blood diseases attack blood cells, but diseases in other parts of the body can also alter blood chemistry. When blood becomes too acid or alkaline, or when it contains an insufficient amount of certain important minerals, especially sodium and potassium, the body can no longer depend on blood as a ready supply of necessary materials for cell functioning. If not corrected, such a chemical imbalance in the blood can lead to serious illness or even death. Often the cause of such an imbalance is sweating that is not compensated for by drinking enough liquids, although chemical imbalances can also be caused by diseases of the kidneys or liver, two organs that regularly adjust conditions in the blood.

Blood cells are manufactured from the stem cells of bone marrow, so conditions that affect these stem cells result in defective blood. Such conditions include several forms of cancer, for which leukemia is the general name, since these cancers mostly affect the white blood cells (*leuke-* means "white"). Red blood cells are subject to genetic disorders and deficiency diseases, classed as anemias. In some diseases chemicals, bacteria, viruses, or parasites interfere with or destroy specific kinds of blood cells or reduce the number of platelets.

A combination of the volume of blood, the activity of the heart, and the condition and activity of the arteries is necessary to maintain enough, but not too much, blood throughout the body. This combination is measured as *blood pressure*. Blood pressure rises and falls with each heartbeat, so it is measured as two numbers, such as 120 over 80. Blood pressure that is too high damages arteries and organs, such as the heart and kidneys, while low blood pressure can cause fainting or, if very low, shock.

Blood poisoning

DISEASE

TYPE: INFECTIOUS
(BACTERIAL)

Phone doctor

The medical name for blood poisoning is *septicemia* (SEHP-tih-SEE-mee-uh) or *sepsis,* or in mild cases, *bacteremia* (BAAK-tuh-REE-mee-uh). Septicemia is not a form of poisoning at all but a bacterial infection that spreads through the circulatory system. In some cases, however, the infecting bacteria do produce a poison (called a *toxin*) as part of their attack on the body. Because the bacteria are being spread by the body's own method for internal transportation, they can reach any organ. As a result, blood poisoning can be very dangerous. ***If blood poisoning is suspected, seek medical attention immediately.***

Cause: Any break in the circulatory system, including a minor cut, can introduce bacteria into the blood. The most serious cases of blood poisoning begin when the break involves a localized sore, such as a boil, that breaks through to the blood. Although many different kinds of bacteria can spread through the blood, the common ones are *Streptococcus* and *Staphylococcus.*

On the Internet
NATIONAL HEALTH SERVICE, UK:
NHS Direct
www.nhsdirect.nhs.uk/
en.aspx?articleid=542

Incidence: Since bacteria are found everywhere, unless a wounded area has been sterilized, they enter blood every time there is a cut. But in most cases the body's immune system quickly defeats invading bacteria. Despite this protection, septicemia is the tenth leading cause of death in the United States. At greatest risk are people over age 65, newborns, and those with AIDS or other problems that compromise the immune system.

Noticeable symptoms: Blood poisoning produces symptoms of shock, including chills and a pale, clammy appearance. There is usually a high fever and sometimes visible eruptions on the skin.

Diagnosis: Blood pressure often falls rapidly in cases of blood poisoning. A physician who suspects septicemia will perform a quick test, called a white-blood-cell count, on a sample of blood. If there are many more white blood cells than usual, it means that the body is fighting an invasion. The blood sample may be cultured to determine the specific bacterium that is causing the disease.

Treatment options: Untreated, septicemia can soon become too severe to stop. In that case, it can be fatal. But if the disease is detected early enough, before progression to shock, antibiotics usually clear it up completely.

The person is hospitalized, given intravenous fluids to maintain blood pressure, and antibiotics to attack the bacteria. A broad-spectrum antibiotic, effective against many kinds of bacteria, is given until the specific kind of bacteria is identified. Then antibiotics specific for that organism are used. Sometimes bacteria become resistant to commonly used antibiotics and a second or even third medicine must be tried.

Prevention and risk factors: Cuts and abrasions should always be washed with soap and water to eliminate as many bacteria as possible, then treated with an antiseptic. Newborns and patients undergoing surgical procedures, including treatment of boils or abscesses, should be monitored for septicemia. Care also must be taken with urinary infections, which often lead to septicemia, either on their own or when a catheter is introduced.

Vaccination to prevent infection by *Hemophilus* (hee-MOF-ih-luhs) *B* bacteria lowers risk. Also, people who have a damaged spleen or who have had the spleen removed should be vaccinated against pneumonia.

Boils

DISEASE

TYPE: INFECTIOUS
(BACTERIAL)

See also
Bacteria and disease
Blood poisoning
Diabetes mellitus, type 1
Diabetes mellitus, type 2
HIV and AIDS

On the Internet
MAYO CLINIC
www.mayoclinic.com/health/
boils-and-carbuncles/DS00466

Phone doctor

A boil is an inflamed, pus-filled swelling of the skin. A cluster of boils connected beneath the skin is called a *carbuncle* (KAAR-buhng-kuhl). Physicians sometimes call boils *furuncles* (FYOO-ruhng-kuhls).

Cause: Boils are caused by certain bacteria, especially *Staphylococcus*. The bacteria usually infect a hair follicle (the cavity in the skin from which the hair grows). White blood cells, which are part of the body's defense system, move into the area to fight the bacteria. This produces white or yellow pus, which consists of white blood cells, bacteria, and dead skin cells.

Incidence: Boils are very common, appearing most often on the face, neck, breasts, and buttocks. Some people who are otherwise healthy develop recurrent boils. Carbuncles also occur in otherwise healthy people. Males frequently develop carbuncles on the back of the neck. People with lowered resistance to infection, including those with diabetes mellitus or AIDS, have an increased susceptibility to carbuncles.

Noticeable symptoms: A boil begins as a red, tender lump. Over the period of one to two days it fills with pus, becoming larger and more painful. Usually it continues to grow for a week or longer, until it bursts.

Sometimes bacteria from a boil enter the blood and are carried to other parts of the body. The spreading infection, called septicemia or blood poisoning, may cause fever, chills, and swollen lymph nodes. ***If this occurs, it is important to see a doctor as soon as possible.*** It also is important to see a doctor if a boil is large or persists for several weeks or more, and if you have recurrent boils, a condition called *furunculosis* (FYOO-ruhng-kuh-LOH-sihs).

Treatment options: Apply warm, damp cloths to the boil several times a day to relieve pain and to hasten bursting and drainage. If a boil is large and painful, a doctor may open it with a sterile needle or knife to drain the pus. If you have recurrent boils, the doctor may prescribe antibiotics and the use of an antiseptic soap.

Bone diseases

On the Internet
MEDLINE PLUS
www.nlm.nih.gov/medlineplus/
bonediseases.html

In addition to well-known injuries such as fractures, bones are susceptible to various diseases. Most of these can develop at any age but they become more common as the body ages.

Although bones contain much calcium and other minerals, they also include living cells in their marrow. Other living cells create the bone that surrounds them. Even the mineral part of bone can be added to or subtracted from by bone cells as the needs of the body change. As a result, any disease or disorder that causes some bones to grow too fast or to lose too much mineral matter results in damage. Furthermore, some diseases of cells in bone adversely affect other parts of the body.

Framework of the body: Just as a modern skyscraper is hung on a framework of steel girders, the body of a human or other vertebrate is supported by a framework of bone. When a disease causes bone to lose or change its mineral content, the damaged framework leads to collapse of part of the body. Bone that is brittle or soft can break easily, for example. When bones in the spine collapse, the spinal cord becomes partly crushed, causing intense pain. In some cases a person visibly shrinks as loss of support causes the body to collapse a little at a time.

The initial processes of development by which bone is formed before birth may be defective for any number of reasons. This may result in bones that are poorly shaped or even absent. Such birth defects range in severity from disfiguring but not life-threatening deformities, such as cleft palate or clubfoot, to conditions that almost invariably lead to death at a very young age.

Bacterial diseases: Bacteria grow almost everywhere, including on bone. The worst damage comes from certain bacteria from diseases that also infect different parts of the body. Such bacteria are often harder to eradicate from bone than from other organs. Tuberculosis is among the bacterial diseases that can infect bone, causing particular damage when the characteristic sores appear on the bones of the spine (*Pott's disease*). Several spirochete bacteria, which cause such diseases as syphilis, Lyme disease, and yaws, are also capable of infecting bone.

Paget's disease: Viruses grow and reproduce only inside living cells, so most viruses do not have the devastating effect on the hard parts of bone that some bacteria do. *Paget's* (PAAJ-ihts) *disease*, however, which may affect as many as 3% of those over 55 in the United States, may be caused by a virus—although no specific culprit has been found. The virus seemingly infects cells that normally release minerals from bone. The infection causes destruction of hard parts of bone, but overcompensation by other types of cells causes bones to thicken. Such thickening may lead to arthritis or even to brain damage if the skull is affected.

For unknown reasons men are more often affected by Paget's disease than women.

Tumors and cancer: Benign tumors can be small and harmless but if they press against nearby tissues they can cause discomfort and other bothersome symptoms. Benign tumors often become cancerous.

Almost all cancer found in bones is secondary cancer. This means that it originates elsewhere, then spreads, or metastasizes (muh-TAAS-tuh-SIYZ-uhz), to the bones. Virtually every kind of cancer can spread to bone but bone metastases (muh-TAAS-tuh-SEEZ) are particularly common in people with advanced breast, lung, or prostate cancer. Bone cancers are very hard to treat.

Cancer that originates in the bones is called primary bone cancer. The main kinds of primary bone cancers are *osteosarcoma* (os-tee-oh-sahr-KOH-muh) and *chondrosarcoma* (KON-droh-sahr-KOH-muh).

Osteosarcoma occurs mainly in children and adults between the ages of 10 and 25. In older patients, it often is a result of Paget's disease. Like other bone cancers, it can develop in any of the body's 206 bones. However, it most often develops in the growing ends of bones around the knee.

Chondrosarcoma typically develops in adults between the ages of 40 and 75. It starts in cartilage that covers the joints of bones and often develops from a benign tumor that has become malignant. The pelvis, thighbone, ribs, and shoulder are the most common sites for the cancer.

Mechanical disorders: Mechanical disorders are caused when physical—not biological or chemical—problems produce a disorder. Bones, both the body's rigid support and system of hinges and bearings, are especially likely candidates for mechanical disorders.

Even healthy bones can break, but they will heal themselves. A physician often must direct the healing process with a splint or cast to ensure that the new bone will grow straight and strong.

Overuse of the body can cause other forms of wear and tear, including *Osgood-Schlatter* (OZ-guud SHLAA-tuhr) *disease,* a partial separation of parts of the knee in young athletes, and osteoarthritis, joint wear in older persons. Mechanical bone problems can often be treated with surgery, including replacement of joints. Obese people may reduce symptoms of osteoarthritis by losing weight.

Some of the "osteo-" disorders

The Greek word for a bone was *osteon,* so the combining form *osteo-* is frequently used in medicine for conditions that affect the bones. It can sometimes be difficult to remember which condition is which, although some are relatively easy to figure out.

- *Osteoarthritis* sounds as if it is "arthritis of the bones." It is a painful condition caused by the wearing away of bone and cartilage at joints. Since it is caused by mechanical wear and tear, it mainly affects older people.
- *Osteoporosis* is also common among older people, especially older women. The word ending *-porosis* is the same base word as *porous.* The name indicates that the bones are becoming porous, or filled with holes, like a sponge. The bones also become brittle and weak. It is thought that the main problem is a lack of calcium in the bones.
- *Osteomalacia* is a condition similar to osteoporosis, but caused by lack of vitamin D. The Greek word *malakia* means softness. Vitamin D is needed to incorporate calcium into bone, so both osteomalacia and osteoporosis are conditions in which there is too little calcium. Sometimes *osteomalacia* is used to mean bone that has lost a different mineral, phosphorous.
- *Osteomyelitis* gets its name by combining the Greek *osteon* with *myel,* a Latin form based on the Greek word for bone marrow, and the familiar medical suffix *-itis,* meaning "inflammation." In osteomyelitis, just as its name indicates, inflammation of the bone marrow is the main problem.
- *Osteosarcoma* (os-tee-oh-sahr-KOH-muh) is a cancer that originates in bone—a sarcoma is a cancer that originates in muscles or connective tissue. Osteosarcoma tends to strike young persons more than older ones—*Ewing's sarcoma* most often attacks the bones of people between the ages of 10 and 20.
- The name *osteogenesis imperfecta* suggests that bone is not completely formed. That is a good inference, since this condition is largely poor formation of cartilage and bone.

Bones

On the Internet
MINNESOTA STATE UNIVERSITY
MANKATO
www.mnsu.edu/emuseum/
biology/humananatomy/skeletal/
skeletalsystem.html

Did You Know?
Analysis of bone marrow cells can help diagnose certain diseases, such as anemia and leukemia. The bone marrow is usually removed from the breastbone or pelvis.

Humans, like other vertebrates, are built around a living framework of bone that grows with them, supporting and protecting the organs of the body. Despite their hardness, bones are often broken, or fractured, in accidents. They can also be affected by many diseases.

There are normally 206 bones in the body, forming the *skeleton*. Bones of the leg can be nearly 2 feet long while the tiny bones of the middle ear are less than an eighth of an inch long. The rest of the skeleton's bones are in between in size.

Bone has two main components. About two-thirds of bone consists of minerals, mostly calcium phosphate, which makes bone hard and resistant to pressure. About one-third of bone is organic matter, mainly collagen, a tough elastic protein that accepts strain and allows for flexibility. Covering the bones is a tough sheath of connective tissue containing a network of blood vessels and nerves. The blood vessels and nerves penetrate the bone through a network of tiny passageways.

Role: Bones support all parts of the body and give it form. They protect many internal organs from injury. For example, the skull protects the brain and the rib cage protects the heart and lungs. Inside bones is a soft tissue called red marrow, which produces most of the body's blood cells. Bones are an important reservoir for minerals such as calcium and phosphorus.

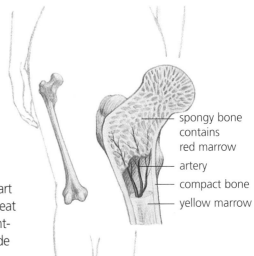

spongy bone contains red marrow
artery
compact bone
yellow marrow

Inside a bone
The spongy-looking inner part of limb bones gives bone great strength combined with lightness, while the marrow inside produces blood cells.

These minerals add strength to bone and can be released into the bloodstream and distributed to other organs as needed.

Growth and maintenance: Healthy bones depend on sufficient minerals and vitamins in the diet. Calcium, phosphorus, fluoride, and other minerals aid bone growth; vitamin C is needed to manufacture collagen. During childhood important hormones promote cell division, thereby stimulating bone growth. Insulin and thyroid hormones are also needed for normal bone growth.

Botulism

(BOCH-uh-LIHZ-uhm)

DISEASE

TYPE: BACTERIAL
       POISONING

See also
Bacteria and disease
Food poisoning

On the Internet
CENTERS FOR DISEASE CONTROL
AND PREVENTION (CDC)
www.cdc.gov/ncidod/dbmd/
diseaseinfo/botulism_g.htm

Eating food contaminated by the botulism bacteria can be fatal. The bacteria themselves are not poisonous. Instead, they produce a highly toxic substance that causes the serious illness.

Cause: Eating improperly prepared canned foods is the most common cause of botulism. That is because the botulism bacterium, *Clostridium botulinum*, grows only in places with no free oxygen gas—such as a sealed can or jar of home preserves.

Spores of botulism bacteria are common in the soil and may cling to raw vegetables or other fresh foods. If the food containing these spores is canned without sufficient boiling, the spores become living botulism bacteria after the can or jar is sealed. As the bacteria multiply in that oxygen-free environment, they give off the powerful toxin that contaminates the food. If the food is eaten, the poison acts on the nervous system by blocking the electrical impulses that make muscles contract. The toxin also causes salivary glands to cease functioning.

In addition to food-borne botulism, three other forms are recognized. Infant botulism strikes babies under 12 months old. Botulism spores in honey or certain other foods lodge in the baby's intestine, where they can become living bacteria and give off their deadly toxin. *Wound botulism*, the rarest form, occurs when spores lodge deep in an unclean wound, multiply, and give off the toxin. The undetermined category includes adult cases in which a specific source cannot be identified.

Incidence: Some cases may go undiagnosed because symptoms are mild. There typically are fewer than 30 reported cases of botulism a year in the United States. Several individuals may become ill at the same time. For instance, one of the largest botulism outbreaks in recent decades involved 28 people who ate at the same restaurant over a period of three days.

Noticeable symptoms: Symptoms generally appear within 36 hours, although some people do not have symptoms for as many as eight days after eating contaminated food. Early signs include abdominal pain, vomiting, headache, blurred or double vision, slurred speech, weakness, constipation, and difficulty in breathing, swallowing, or speaking. Infant botulism has similar symptoms plus characteristic "floppy baby" loss of head control. ***Botulism can be fatal if medical treatment is delayed. Get immediate medical attention.***

Call ambulance

Diagnosis: Based on respiratory problems and other symptoms, a physician may suspect botulism poisoning. Examination can reveal paralyzed eye or throat muscles. A blood test can confirm this diagnosis by showing toxin in the blood, but sometimes it is necessary to perform additional tests to rule out other possible causes of paralysis.

Treatment options: Treatment should begin as soon as possible. An emergency medical service (EMS) should be called immediately. If you know cardiopulmonary resuscitation (CPR), it should be practiced to keep oxygen flowing into the lungs if breathing difficulties appear while waiting for EMS. Anyone who has eaten the suspected food, whether showing symptoms or not, should be given emergency care.

Doctors induce vomiting to clear out any contaminated food in the stomach and flush out the patient's intestinal tract. An antitoxin for botulism helps counter the effects of the poison. If muscle paralysis is severe, a respirator may be needed to help with breathing.

More than three out of four persons who develop botulism poisoning eventually recover completely with proper care.

Use CPR

Prevention: Food-borne botulism is highest among people who can their own foods. Good food-preparation and hygiene rules should be followed whenever preparing, storing, and preserving food. Food in cans that are swollen or dented should never be eaten. Many foods are packaged in cans with special pop tops; if the top pops up, the food is contaminated. ***If you suspect any canned food could be bad, throw it away.***

Boiling breaks down botulism toxins, so canned foods should be heated to boiling prior to serving. Never give infants unpasteurized honey. Carefully wash out wounds with soap and water, and apply a bacteria-killing medicine to deep wounds.

Botulism and Botox

In its purest form, botulism toxin is one of the deadliest poisons known. However, injections of tiny amounts of sterile, purified toxin have both therapeutic and cosmetic uses. Known as Botox, the toxin interferes with the functions of nerves that control muscles or other structures. For example, Botox is used to treat overactive bladder, a condition caused by spasms of the muscles that control the urinary bladder. Other uses include treating migraine headaches, excessive underarm sweating, and an eye disorder characterized by excessive blinking. But the best-known and most popular use of Botox injections is by plastic surgeons to erase facial wrinkles, temporarily improving a person's appearance. There is no chance of contracting botulism from these injections, but occasionally there are complications such as facial pain or droopy eyelid muscles.

Bowel obstruction

DISEASE

TYPE: MECHANICAL

See also
Back and spine problems
Digestive system
Gallstones
Hernias
Ileitis
Kidney and bladder stones
Large intestine
Peritonitis
Pregnancy and disease
Small intestine
Tumor, benign

Bowel obstruction, also known as *ileus* (IHL-ee-uhs), is the stoppage of onward movement of the food-derived materials passing through the intestine. It results from any kind of blockage or from spasms or paralysis of a part of the intestine. The onset of ileus occurs infrequently, but its onset often requires emergency treatment.

Cause: Bowel obstruction can result from any of three causes.

■ Any sort of mechanical blockage or obstruction, including *adhesion* following surgery—an adhesion is a joining together of two parts of the body by scar tissue. The intestine may become bent back or twisted, an obstruction termed a *volvulus* (VOL-vyuh-luhs). A stone from the gallbladder, or even something indigestible that was eaten, can enter and block the intestine.

■ Pressure on the intestine from an adjacent organ, most commonly a uterus distended by pregnancy. Other possible blockages of this type include a hernia through which the intestine protrudes or a tumor that presses on the intestine.

On the Internet
MEDLINE PLUS
www.nlm.nih.gov/medlineplus/
ency/article/000260.htm

■ Any breakdown in normal functioning of the intestine, such as muscular paralysis or spasm or nerve impairment, stops the intestinal action that moves material onward. Such nerve impairment may appear in connection with peritonitis, complications with kidney stones or gallstones, or injury to the spinal cord.

Noticeable symptoms: Sharp pain in the abdomen coming first in spasms but later as uninterrupted pain is one of the first signs of bowel obstruction. Other signs include constipation, vomiting (which may include feces), and swelling of the abdomen. Severe dehydration and shock can develop not long after the outbreak of symptoms unless the condition is relieved by prompt treatment.

Diagnosis: Applying a stethoscope to the abdomen will reveal to a doctor the absence of any bowel sounds in a person with ileus. Such bowel sounds are constantly present in normal health. Abdominal x-rays of someone with bowel obstruction usually exhibit curved portions of intestine badly swollen by ballooning gases.

Treatment: Prompt treatment of bowel obstruction to relieve intestinal pressure is important in order to prevent perforation of the intestinal wall. ***A person with ileus should not eat or drink.*** Essential body fluids normally provided by intestinal action may need to be supplied intravenously.

No food

A usual first step in treatment is to pump out the contents of the stomach. Intestinal pressure may be relieved by applying suction through a tube to the obstruction. This procedure may be sufficient to restore intestinal functioning that has been interrupted by a cause such as paralysis. Surgery may eventually be necessary in order to clear an obstruction.

Brain

BODY SYSTEM

Thought by some ancient Greeks to be merely an "air conditioner" for the blood, the brain is known today as the main part of the central nervous system, controlling all parts of the body. The brain also records and interprets information from the senses, stores that information in itself as memory, participates in emotions, and in humans at least, thinks. If a human were a computer, the brain would be all of the chips, from the memory chips to the central processing unit.

On the Internet
HOW STUFF WORKS
www.howstuffworks.com/
brain.htm

Size and location: Located in the head, the brain is protected by the bones of the skull. There are two parts to the brain, called *hemispheres*. Each hemisphere is about 6 inches long from the front of the head to the back. The distance across the pair from left to right is about 4½ inches. Below the hemispheres a single *brain stem*, about 3 inches long, connects the brain to the *spinal cord*, which is connected to most of the rest of the nervous system. The nerves of the head, however, are connected directly to the brain. The brain itself weighs about 3 pounds.

Role: The brain is composed of several parts. The *cerebrum* (SEHR-uh-bruhm) is the folded outer part of each hemisphere. Its outer layer, the *cerebral cortex* (SEHR-uh-bruhl KAWR-tehks), governs thought, the senses, and movement. The cerebral cortex is less than 0.25-inch thick but deeply folded, so that if it were spread out flat, it would be about a yard square.

The two hemispheres of the *cerebellum* (SEHR-uh-BEHL-uhm) control balance and muscle coordination. The two halves of the brain are connected by the *corpus callosum* (kuh-LOH-suhm). Deep in the brain the brain stem governs involuntary muscles. A small, but important, part of the brain is the *hypothalamus* (HIY-poh-THAAL-uh-muhs), which controls the hormonal system. Various other small regions in the brain that have specific functions have been identified.

Conditions that affect the brain: Almost any disease affects the brain to some degree, but for most diseases the effect is indirect: pain and fatigue caused by disease, for example, are felt in the brain, manifested as headache or mental weariness. A sort of fence, called the *blood-brain barrier*, keeps many agents of disease and their products from reaching the brain itself.

The heavy skull is designed to protect the brain from injury, but often a sharp blow can bruise the brain against the inside of the skull; or the skull may be broken, and part of the bone or swelling can press against the brain. Any pressure or damage to the brain interferes with its function. Memories may be lost, limbs may become paralyzed, or death may result from damage to different parts of the brain.

The two hemispheres of the brain have been mapped. Different parts of the cerebrum handle different responses to the environment. The corpus callosum connects the hemispheres. Deep in the brain the hypothalamus controls body temperature, appetite, and the nearby pituitary gland, which in turn uses its hormone production to influence growth, energy use, sexual development, and reproduction.

HEMISPHERES of CEREBRUM

senses
movement
behavior and emotion
hands
personality
thought
speech
hearing
smell
vision
memory

CEREBELLUM

skull
cerebrum
corpus callosum
hypothalamus
pituitary gland

cerebellum
brain stem
spinal cord

The nervous system, including the brain, uses chemical messengers to communicate with its different parts. Too much or too little of a particular messenger in the brain can cause serious disease, including some severe mental illnesses called *psychoses* (siy-KOH-seez).

Development of the brain can be affected in various ways. Some genetic disorders impair the formation of the brain to one degree or another, often during the fetal stages of growth, but sometimes well into adulthood. A few diseases, such as rubella or alcoholism, and some vitamin deficiencies in a mother can also interfere with fetal development of the brain. When the brain is affected before birth or in early years, mental ability may be impaired.

Did You Know?

People long ago had many ideas about the functions of various organs. In ancient Greece, Hippocrates believed that the brain was the seat of intelligence and involved with the senses. But Aristotle believed the heart was the center of intelligence and thought.

Brain abscess

DISEASE

TYPE: MECHANICAL

See also
Abscess
Bacteria and disease
Brain
Dental illnesses and conditions

Call ambulance

On the Internet
MEDLINE PLUS
www.nlm.nih.gov/medlineplus/
ency/article/000783.htm

A brain abscess is an area inside the brain filled with pus. The abscess often has a skin, called a capsule, surrounding it. A growing abscess is dangerous and produces many of its symptoms by the pressure it exerts on nearby regions of the brain.

Cause: A brain abscess begins when bacteria or other microorganisms somehow get into the brain and multiply. Most abscesses begin with an infection in other parts of the body, usually the sinuses, middle ear, teeth, or jaw. Sometimes infections in the chest or lungs travel to the brain, and sometimes a brain abscess results from a wound to the skull.

Noticeable symptoms: Most people with a brain abscess have a headache that does not go away. They may also have mild fever, seizures, nausea, or a stiff neck, usually several together. Depending on the location of the abscess in the brain, speech, movement, or balance may be affected, with symptoms similar to those of a stroke. *A brain abscess is a medical emergency; the patient should get to the emergency room of a hospital as soon as possible.*

Diagnosis: Since many of the symptoms of a brain abscess can have other causes, a physician will ask about recent travel and known infections to eliminate specific diseases that would require a different treatment. After the physician rules out other causes, a CT scan and probably a CT-directed biopsy of the brain (a procedure to remove and examine directly tissue from the brain) will be performed to make a specific diagnosis.

Treatment: Two types of treatment are usually combined. Antibiotics are prescribed to cure the infection, and the abscess is physically removed by a surgical procedure. Often intravenous antibiotics will be administered even before the diagnosis is certain, since halting the infection is vital. After an abscess has been located, a surgeon will cut the abscess out or use aspiration to suck out the diseased material.

The combination treatment is very effective. Approximately 90% of people with a brain abscess survive. Half of the survivors, however, have continuing problems related to the damage the abscess causes to the brain, which may include seizures or personality changes.

Risk factors: About 25% of all brain abscesses occur in children with congenital heart disease or a defect that makes it easier for infections to reach the brain from elsewhere in the body. Other risk factors include chronic middle ear and sinus infections, dental or jaw infections, meningitis, head injuries, and infections of the face or scalp. Drug abuse and diseases that harm the immune system, such as AIDS, also increase risk.

Prevention: The chances of developing brain abscesses may be reduced by prompt treatment of any infections that can cause them. This includes sinus infections, ear infections, and other infections of the face and jaw. Good dental hygiene, including regular flossing and brushing, is important, since a gum abscess may break through to become a brain abscess. People with congenital or rheumatic heart disease or with surgical implants (such as an artificial hip) should be given preventative antibiotics before undergoing dental or urological procedures.

Breakbone fever

See **Dengue fever**

Breast cancer

DISEASE

TYPE: CANCER

See also
Cancers
Fibrocystic breast disease
Genetic diseases
Hormonal system

On the Internet
MEDLINE PLUS
www.nlm.nih.gov/medlineplus/
breastcancer.html

Not all breast lumps are cancerous. Most are benign, or noncancerous. But all lumps should be treated with suspicion. Breast cancer can be fatal, but with early detection and treatment most patients survive.

Types: Like other cancers, those that develop in the breast are characterized by the uncontrolled growth and spread of abnormal cells.

There are various types of breast cancer. Noninvasive types are confined to the milk-producing glands and their ducts. Invasive types have spread into the fatty tissue of the breast. There are non-inherited forms and inherited forms caused by either the *BRCA1* or *BRCA2* gene. Estrogen, the female hormone, encourages the growth of some tumors, while other tumors are estrogen-negative.

Cause: Research indicates that the development of breast cancer is a highly complex process. Over a period of years, even decades, a series of genetic errors occur. This accumulation of mutations, genetic duplications, and rearrangements of genetic material eventually set off uncontrollable cell growth and enable cells to keep dividing forever.

Various factors have been implicated in the process. People who inherit the *BRCA1* or *BRCA2* gene are most susceptible. Certain behaviors, such as smoking, and certain environmental factors, such as exposure to radiation, increase the chance that breast cancer will develop. In mice an infectious virus causes breast cancer; it is possible that a similar virus exists in humans.

Incidence: Each year more than 200,000 Americans are diagnosed with invasive breast cancer, and about 40,000 die from the disease. The incidence of new cases increased in recent decades, but the death rates declined thanks to early detection and powerful new drugs. The great majority of breast cancer cases occur in women, but each year about 1,700 cases are diagnosed in men. Inherited forms of breast cancer account for 5 to 10% of new cases.

In Canada, more than 20,000 women develop breast cancer annually and over 5,000 die of the disease. Worldwide, more than 1 million women are diagnosed with the disease each year. Incidence rates vary considerably, with the highest rates in the developed world and the lowest rates in Africa and Asia.

Noticeable symptoms: Most breast cancers are found during self-examination. The patient feels or sees a lump in or near the breast or in the underarm area. Other common signs include thickening or distortion of the breast, a discharge from the nipple, and skin irritation or discoloration.

To do a self exam, with your hands on your waist, press inward and raise your shoulders. Turn from side to side and look for any differences between breasts, especially sores, nipple changes, or discharge. Raise your hands above your head and repeat the comparison.

A good time to complete the examination is after a bath, running wet, soapy hands along the breasts to feel for any lumps or thickening. This can be started while standing, but a more detailed examination should be completed while lying on your back, preferably with a pillow under the arm below the breast being examined. Move fingers to the nipple first and then away in a circular motion, making sure that the whole breast is covered. Also squeeze and then depress the nipple to watch for discharge and to feel for lumps under it.

Breast self-examination

About 90% of all breast cancers are found by women themselves. A regular monthly self-examination leads to early detection, important both for safety and for reducing the amount of surgery that might be required in case cancer is detected.

Diagnosis: During an examination, a physician will carefully feel the breast for masses and examine the breast surface for any skin changes or other abnormalities. If a suspicious lump is detected or if a *mammogram* (a low-dose x-ray of the breast) finds an abnormal area, a *biopsy* will be performed. In this procedure a small amount of tissue is removed from the suspect area and examined under a microscope. Cancer cells look markedly different from normal cells. Other tests can determine if the tumor is estrogen-positive and how rapidly the tumor cells are dividing.

Stages and progress: Determining the stage of the cancer is critical for choosing the most effective treatment. Staging describes the size of the tumor and whether it has spread to nearby lymph nodes or to other organs. A widely used staging system assigns a category of I, II, III, or IV. I is an early stage, with no indication that the cancer has spread beyond the breast. IV is the most advanced stage, with the cancer having spread, or *metastasized* (muh-TAAST-uh-SIYZD), to distant sites such as bones or to lymph nodes not near the breast. The more advanced the cancer, the more difficult it is to treat.

Treatment options: The plan of treatment recommended by a physician depends on the stage of the cancer, the patient's general health, and the patient's preferences. Conventional options are surgery, radiation, and chemotherapy. Often all three are used. Surgery may involve the complete removal of the breast in a *mastectomy* (maa-STEHK-tuh-mee). Or only the tumor and nearby tissue may be removed in a *lumpectomy* (luhm-PEHK-tuh-mee). Generally, one or more lymph nodes under the adjacent arm are removed to determine if fragments of the tumor have spread to the nodes.

Radiation therapy, or radiotherapy, uses high-energy x-rays to kill cancer cells. Chemotherapy uses drugs to kill cancer cells. Both radiation and chemotherapy harm normal cells and have unpleasant short-term side effects.

Following primary treatment, many breast cancer patients take either tamoxifen or Femara. These drugs work against tumors sensitive to estrogen, significantly lowering the risk of breast cancer recurrence.

Prevention and early detection: Various practices have been suggested as being helpful in reducing the risk of breast cancer. These include regular exercise, a low-fat diet, maintaining a healthy weight, and avoiding alcohol and tobacco. Hormone replacement therapy, sometimes prescribed to women during menopause, increases risk.

There is no guaranteed way to prevent breast cancer. A woman's best recourse is early detection through self-examination and regular mammograms—x-ray pictures that can find tumors up to two years or more before they are large enough to be felt. The American Cancer Society recommends that women ages 20 to 39 have their breasts examined by a health-care professional every three years; women age 40 and older should have an annual mammogram and clinical examination. All women should examine their breasts once a month.

Bright's disease	*See* **Kidney diseases**
Broken bones	*See* **Fractures, strains, and sprains**

Bronchitis

(brong-KIY-tihs)

DISEASE

TYPE: INFECTIOUS (VIRAL)
OR ENVIRONMENTAL

See also
Asthma
Common cold
COPD
   (chronic obstructive
   pulmonary disease)
Coughs
Cystic fibrosis
Emphysema
Environment and disease
Lungs
Measles (rubeola)
Nose and throat conditions
Pertussis
Tobacco and disease
Viruses and disease

On the Internet
MEDLINE PLUS
www.nlm.nih.gov/medlineplus/
bronchitis.html

Don't smoke

Avoid aspirin

Young children who have recently had a bad cold or older people who have smoked tobacco for many years are most likely to experience an attack of a lung and throat disorder called bronchitis. Others may develop infections that attack the bronchial tubes that also are termed bronchitis.

Cause: *Acute infectious bronchitis* is caused by a viral infection of the bronchi (BRONG-kiy)—the air passages that lead from the throat to the lungs. *Chronic bronchitis* is more often environmental, occurring when the bronchi are repeatedly irritated by tobacco smoke or air pollution.

Acute infectious bronchitis is most likely to occur in winter and in children after a viral disease such as a cold, measles, or whooping cough. Active or passive cigarette smoking, air pollution, lung infections, or abnormal growth of the bronchi are the main causes of chronic bronchitis in adults. Chronic bronchitis usually accompanies emphysema, a serious lung disease of the air sacs.

Incidence: An estimated 12 million Americans may have chronic bronchitis. It is especially common in smokers over 40 years of age.

Noticeable symptoms: Symptoms of both acute and chronic bronchitis include a cough that releases mucous secretions from the lungs called *sputum* (SPYOO-tuhm), breathlessness or wheezing, fever, chest pain upon coughing, soreness, and back pain.

Diagnosis: A physician will listen with a stethoscope for abnormal sounds, called rales (RAHLZ), from the lungs as a breath is taken. Chest x-rays give the physician a more accurate determination of the affected airways and can be used to rule out other lung diseases. A lung test (blowing into a tube) measures lung capacity. For chronic bronchitis a blood test can measure oxygen in the blood.

Treatment options: Treatment for both acute and chronic bronchitis attacks includes bed rest, lots of fluids, medication to reduce fever, antibiotics if a secondary bacterial infection attacks the lungs, and nebulizers to help remove mucus from airways. Expectorant cough medicines, not suppressants, are recommended for treating the characteristic bronchitis cough. Aspirin is not recommended for reducing fever in young people because its use can induce *Reye's syndrome.*

Prevention: The safest course of action is to avoid smoking and breathing polluted air, smoke, dust, or fumes. Cold or damp environments also contribute to the disease. Eating a well-balanced diet, drinking enough fluids, and staying away from people who have viral infections also help.

Brucellosis	*See* **Animal diseases and humans**
Bruises	*See* **Bleeding and bruises**

Bruxism
(BRUK-sihz-uhm)

SYMPTOM

TYPE: MECHANICAL; MENTAL

See also
Dental illnesses and conditions
Stress
Teeth

Practice meditation

Bruxism is the grinding or clenching of teeth. It is an unintentional, subconscious behavior, occurring most often while the person sleeps. Many people with bruxism are unaware of the problem until someone else points it out or until they see the physical damage caused by the habit.

Parts affected: Clenching the jaws together and grinding the lower teeth against the upper teeth causes excessive wear on the teeth. The teeth and fillings may be chipped, broken, or loosened. As the tooth enamel is ground off, the teeth become sensitive to cold, pressure, and other stimuli. Lack of enamel also leads to tooth decay. Receding gums may occur, and in extreme cases the teeth are worn down to stumps. The grinder also may experience headaches, earaches, hearing loss, and sore facial muscles.

Cause: A variety of factors may trigger or exacerbate bruxism. These include emotional stress and nervous tension, smoking, alcohol, antidepressant drugs, vitamin or mineral deficiencies, tooth fillings and other dental procedures, and mouth injuries. Young children may grind their teeth in response to the discomfort of ailments such as colds, allergies, and ear infections.

Treatment options: Bruxism is most common in children. Fortunately, juvenile bruxism usually disappears spontaneously. Treatment is needed only when the habit persists.

When a dentist sees signs of bruxism, the patient's medical history and habits are reviewed. Patients are advised to reduce stress, perhaps by trying psychotherapy or yoga, and

Avoid alcohol

Don't smoke

to eliminate use of alcohol and tobacco. If an antidepressant is a suspected cause, reducing the dose or switching to another antidepressant may be recommended.

The dentist helps the patient learn how to position the teeth and tongue properly. If necessary, a customized mouth guard is made to be worn while sleeping. The mouth guard absorbs the punishment that would otherwise be endured by the teeth, thereby reducing further damage to the teeth.

Bubonic plague	*See* **Plague**
Buerger's disease	*See* **Circulatory system; Veins**

Bulimia
(boo-LIHM-ee-uh)

DISEASE

TYPE: EATING DISORDER

See also
Anorexia nervosa
Constipation
Diet and health
Hemorrhoids
Nausea
Obesity

On the Internet
KIDS HEALTH
kidshealth.org/teen/food_fitness/
problems/eat_disorder.html

Bulimia, or *bulimia nervosa,* is a serious eating disorder characterized by episodes of binge eating alternating with self-induced vomiting, purging (using laxatives to promote bowel evacuation), excessive exercising, or a combination of those behaviors. The purpose of the vomiting, purging, and exercise is to avoid the weight gain induced by binging. Like the eating disorder anorexia nervosa, which is characterized by reducing food intake to tiny amounts, bulimia most often occurs in teenage girls and young women. People experiencing bulimia typically have distorted self-images and other deep-seated psychological problems. The word *bulimic* is sometimes used to describe a person with bulimia.

Cause: Doctors do not know why some people develop the eating disorder bulimia, but family pressures and profound psychological problems are thought to play a role. Like people with anorexia nervosa, those with bulimia tend to have parents who are achievement oriented and controlling. Diet and slimness often are important topics of family conversation and so figure in the patient's sense of self-esteem.

Those with bulimia frequently have a history of being overweight. Thus bulimia may be viewed as a form of overcompensation. People with bulimia also tend to be somewhat older than those with anorexia and more frequently exhibit antisocial and compulsive behavior patterns along with their eating disorder.

One of the key signs of bulimia is the food binge—eating a large amount of a high-calorie food in a short period of time. This is frequently followed by vomiting or purging along with feelings of guilt for the behavior that may lead to a period of self-imposed fasting. But after a time the feelings subside, and another binge is started.

Incidence: Bulimia usually occurs in young females from middle- or upper-class families. It is believed to be more common than anorexia, possibly affecting up to 19% of college-age women. Reports of incidence vary widely though; some suggest as few as 3% of young women are bulimics.

In addition to young women, ballet dancers, gymnasts, jockeys, and wrestlers are vulnerable to bulimia. People with these professions or hobbies need to keep their weight low to be successful. But instead of maintaining a regular regimen of dieting and exercise, the performer or athlete with bulimia loses control of diet and then overcompensates in a harmful way.

Noticeable symptoms: Though bulimics may rapidly gain or lose, they usually remain within 20% of their normal weight. The classic symptom is the eating binge, although an observer would see this only by chance. People with bulimia nearly always gorge themselves secretly. They may embark on several different eating binges each day for several days at a time before purging themselves with laxatives or with self-induced vomiting. Medicines called *diuretics* (DIY-uh-REHT-ihks) may be used to promote urination, and thus temporarily lower weight through loss of fluids. A period of self-imposed starvation or excessive exercise may follow an episode of binging.

A bulimic's dentist or dental hygienist may be the first person to notice the disorder. Over time the bulimic's excessive vomiting may erode tooth enamel and dentin, giving teeth a smooth glassy appearance, causing decay, and increasing susceptibility to serious nerve infections. Dry mouth, due to a lack of saliva resulting from abuse of laxatives or diuretics, or dehydration due to vomiting, is another symptom.

Diagnosis: A doctor will want to make certain that the suspected disorder is bulimia and not another recently recognized eating problem, *binge eating disorder.* Binge eating, which is more common than bulimia, involves eating abnormal amounts of food and leads to significant weight gain. Low self-esteem and depression are among the possible causes. Binge eating is not accompanied by frantic attempts to undo the excess intake.

The periodic binging and purging of a person with bulimia eventually affect the patient's body in a variety of ways. Stomach acid passes through the mouth during repeated vomiting, leaving teeth sharp and rough. Acid also irritates and inflames the esophagus and pharynx, giving the bulimic a puffy-cheeked appearance. Laxative abuse often causes hemorrhoids and chronic constipation by upsetting normal rhythms of the digestive tract. Vomiting can cause dehydration and electrolyte imbalances, as can diuretic and laxative abuse. But unlike women with anorexia, bulimic women do not lose their periods because they usually remain close to their normal body weight.

Treatment options: Early diagnosis and treatment of bulimia are important because the longer the disorder continues, the more difficult treatment becomes. Bulimics can be treated on an outpatient basis to help them restore control over eating habits. A doctor may prescribe an antidepressant such as fluoxetine and may have the patient take part in individual and group therapy. This can allow the bulimic to begin confronting the underlying personal and family problems that helped bring on the disorder.

Even though patients show clear signs of progress in dealing with their eating and emotional problems, psychiatric counseling and physical checkups often continue on a regular basis for months or longer. About 74% of bulimics recover fully with treatment, and 99% achieve at least partial recovery.

Stages and progress: Bulimia usually begins with dieting to lose weight. But some girls and young women lose control over the craving for food that dieting brings and suddenly eat large amounts of high-calorie foods in a matter of hours. Following this, or after other similar binges, the binger suffers guilt and self-recrimination for having lost control, combined with the fear of becoming overweight. Then purging, perhaps with the use of diuretics, and self-induced vomiting begin. A period of self-inflicted starvation or extreme dieting often follows until the next episode of binge eating.

Those with bulimia generally do not suffer the severe physical effects that those with anorexia do, and death from bulimia is rare. Frequent purging can cause heart damage, however, and acid in the throat may contribute to later development of cancer.

Breaking the binge-purge cycle can be difficult, especially if underlying psychological problems are severe.

Burns and scalds

Phone doctor

Most people burn themselves sooner or later; however, most burns are minor and heal naturally.

Cause: Burns are caused by contact with high heat or flames, electricity, chemicals, or exposure to the sun. Scalds are burns caused by contact with hot liquids or steam.

Incidence: It is estimated that more than a million burns or scalds require medical attention annually in the United States alone. About 50,000 of these burns or scalds cause the victim to be hospitalized, half in special burn-treatment units. Each year about 4,500 Americans die from burns or scalds directly, while lowered immune defense caused by burns or scalds contributes to pneumonia or other infections that lead to somewhat more than that number of deaths.

Noticeable symptoms: Burns are classified according to their degree of seriousness.

- *First-degree burns* are the least serious. They are often caused by contact with hot objects or scalding. Symptoms include redness, mild swelling, and pain. These burns usually heal by themselves. Most sunburns are first-degree burns.
- *Second-degree burns* are often caused by direct contact with very hot liquids. They can also result from contact with gasoline, kerosene, and chemicals. Symptoms of second-degree burns include red or blotchy skin, blisters, and swelling. Second-degree burns are noticeably wet. This wetness results when plasma, the liquid part of blood, seeps out through the damaged skin layers. Severe sunburns are second-degree burns.
- *Third-degree burns* occur when the heat is at a high temperature or the contact is long. They might result from direct contact with flames, chemicals, or electricity, or from immersion in hot water. With third-degree burns all skin layers are destroyed, resulting in a charred grayish appearance. A person with a third-degree burn will not feel pain because the nerve endings have been destroyed.

Diagnosis: Your physician will note the extent of damage to skin, fat, and muscle. He or she will also look for symptoms of dehydration and for infections that may occur as a result of the burns.

Simple safety habits can prevent most burns from happening in the first place.

Treatment options: The type of treatment needed depends on four things: (1) the seriousness of the burn (2) the amount of the body burned (3) the parts of the body burned, and (4) the substance that caused the burn. These are detailed in the table at the bottom of the page.

Minor burns usually do not need medical attention, but first-aid steps as outlined on the next page are helpful. More serious second-degree burns and all third-degree burns must be treated by a physician. First aid should be applied immediately, however, without waiting for the physician.

The physician may prescribe antibiotics or an antibacterial ointment. Severe burns may require hospitalization, where treatment may include replacing lost liquids, either orally or intravenously, and therapy for shock. For third-degree burns skin grafts, using healthy skin from elsewhere on the body or the application of artificial skin, may be necessary.

Prevention: The best way to prevent burns is to avoid the type of accidents that lead to burns. Make sure that electrical appliances are cared for and used properly. Avoid chemical burns by carefully following instructions on products that contain potentially dangerous substances. Wear protective gear such as gloves and eye goggles when handling chemicals. Avoid keeping flammable materials such as gasoline or paint thinners at home, but always have smoke alarms and fire extinguishers in the home.

Degrees of Burn Danger

Type	Degree	Extent of Burn and Body Parts Burned
Minor	All first-degree and some second-degree burns	Less than 15%* of the body for adults and less than 10% for children and the elderly
Severe	Most second-degree burns	10 to 25% of the body for adults and 10 to 20% for children and the elderly; electrical burns are also termed severe
Critical	Some second-degree and all third-degree burns	More than 25% of the body for adults and more than 20% for children and the elderly; second- or third-degree burns of face, hands, eyes, or feet

*One percent of the body is about the size of the victim's open hand.

First aid for burns

Place *minor and severe burns* in cold water for up to 45 minutes to lessen the pain. Then gently blot the burned area dry. Wrap severe burns in a clean cloth or bandage. Do not break the blisters or remove loose pieces of skin. You may take aspirin or acetaminophen (Tylenol) or apply aloe vera creams to relieve the pain. **Do not spread butter or other oils over the wound.** This folk remedy holds in the heat instead of cooling the burn.

Do not place critical burns in cold water since the cold may cause hypothermia, or below-normal body temperature. Do cover them with a clean cloth or sterile dressing. People with critical burns might also need treatment for shock.

For *chemical burns* follow the directions on the container the substance came in. In the container's absence remove clothing and jewelry and wash the burn with water for 15 to 20 minutes. (If the burn is from a dry chemical, brush the chemical off before removing clothing and jewelry.)

If the eye has been injured by intense heat, run water over it while it is open for at least 15 minutes. Then cover it with a sterile dressing.

Bursitis

(bur-SIY-tuhs)

DISEASE

TYPE: MECHANICAL;
      INFECTION
      (BACTERIAL)

See also
Gout
Inflammation
Rheumatoid arthritis
"Staph"
Tennis elbow and related problems

The body has 156 fluid-filled sacs, or bursas; most are located in joints, where they act as cushions to minimize friction. An inflammation of a bursa is called bursitis.

Parts affected: Any bursa may become inflamed. Joints that are particularly susceptible to bursitis include those in the shoulder, elbow, hip, knee, ankle, and big toe.

Cause: Bursitis is usually caused by excessive trauma. It typically results from an injury or from a repeated physical activity. Bursitis may be precipitated by certain types of arthritis, such as rheumatoid arthritis, or gout. It also may result from infection, usually by the bacterium *Staphylococcus aureus*.

Noticeable symptoms: Bursitis is often accompanied by pain, redness, and swelling of the area around the inflamed bursa. One's ability to move the joint may be limited.

Associations: Bursitis in the shoulder is the most common form, but bursas become sore at other locations as well. One cause of "tennis elbow" is an inflammation of the bursa that develops when the elbow is overused (inflammation of the tendons in that joint is also called tennis elbow). "Housemaid's knee" is an inflammation of the bursa at the front of the knee that results from excessive kneeling. "Weaver's bottom," an inflammation of a bursa in the hip area, is caused by prolonged sitting on hard surfaces. Continued pressure on a bunion (a misplaced joint in a toe), perhaps from tight-fitting shoes, can cause bursitis.

Stages and progress: Bursitis often clears up within a week, particularly if the aggravating condition is avoided, and the inflamed joint is rested. However, if you have recently injured a joint or if the pain is severe or lasts more than one week, it is advisable to see a doctor.

Treatment options: Common anti-inflammatory drugs such as aspirin or ibuprofen often relieve pain and swelling. In severe cases a physician may inject a corticosteroid medication into the affected area. The doctor will usually suggest exercises to help prevent the formation of scar tissue. If a bursa becomes infected or if it is subject to repeated inflammations, surgery may be necessary.

Caisson disease	*See* **Bends**
Calluses and corns	*See* **Foot problems**

Cancers

DISEASE

TYPE: GENETIC;
ENVIRONMENTAL;
VIRAL

A generation or two ago the word *cancer* was avoided in polite conversation. The diseases collectively known as cancer seemed at that time too horrible and too surely fatal to discuss. But people's attitudes have changed, thanks to three factors: a much better understanding of how cancers develop, greatly improved treatments, and the knowledge that millions of people have survived bouts of cancer to lead healthy lives.

Cause: Cancer can be considered a genetic disease, even though it is very different from diseases usually grouped in this category. The underlying cause of all cancers is errors in the genetic material DNA (deoxyribonucleic acid), the large molecule that is composed of genes. These errors, or mutations, may be present at birth or may develop any time thereafter.

DNA is thought of primarily in terms of heredity but it also has a critical day-to-day function: It directs production of the proteins that carry out all operations of each cell. Alterations in DNA can disrupt these operations. If alterations interfere with the processes by which cells grow and reproduce, abnormally high numbers of cells may be created. The cells form a mass, or tumor. Some tumors are benign. Their growth is limited and they remain localized. Warts are examples of benign tumors. In contrast, cancerous tumors are said to be malignant. They are characterized by uncontrolled cell growth and proliferation, and by the tendency to spread, or metastasize (muh-TAAS-tuh-SIYZ), throughout the body.

Cancers are classed by the type of tissue in which they originate. *Carcinomas* (KAHR-suh-NOH-muhz) originate in the inner or outer linings of organs. *Sarcomas* (sahr-KOH-muhz) form in muscle or bone. *Leukemias* (loo-KEE-mee-uhz) affect blood-forming cells in bone marrow. *Lymphomas* (lihm-FOH-muhz) develop in lymph tissue.

Many different pathways can lead to cancer. Some people are born with genes that increase the risk of developing cancer. For example, women who inherit either the *BRCA1* or *BRCA2* gene have an increased risk of breast cancer. Mutations, or changes, in genes can also increase cancer risk. Certain genes, called tumor suppressor genes, regulate cell growth and division. Mutations in these genes can result in uncontrolled cell growth. Other genes, called oncogenes, are normally inactive, but if activated by mutations they initiate cancerous growth.

Environmental factors can cause mutations. Chemicals, especially those in tobacco and tobacco smoke, are known to cause cancer. Radiation, including radioactivity and ultraviolet rays in sunlight, damages DNA. Viruses disrupt the normal pattern of cell growth and reproduction; indeed, it is estimated that each year 17% of new cancers worldwide are attributable to infection. For example, the major causes of liver cancer are infection with the hepatitis B or hepatitis C virus.

It can take a dozen or more mutations to cause a cancer. Thus, it can take many years for a person to accumulate the mutations needed to form a tumor. This explains why the incidence of cancer increases with age.

Incidence: Cancer is the second leading cause of death in the United States, after heart disease. However, heart disease deaths have declined dramatically in recent decades while cancer deaths have declined only slightly. This decline would be much greater if it were not for the increasing age of the nation's population, since incidence of cancer rises with age. According to the American Cancer Society, approximately 76% of all cancers are diagnosed in people age 55 and older.

In 2005 over 1.3 million new cancer cases were diagnosed in the United States, and about 570,000 persons died, nearly all from cancers diagnosed in previous years. The deaths account for about one of every four deaths in the nation. This is also true in Canada, which has an estimated 149,000 new cases of cancer and 69,500 cancer-related deaths annually.

American males have slightly less than a one in three life-time risk of developing cancer; females have slightly more than a one in three risk. The leading sites of newly detected cancers are the prostate in men and the breasts in women. However, the nation's leading cause of cancer deaths is lung cancer. It is the second most commonly diagnosed type of cancer each year but it accounts for about 30% of all cancer deaths annually. Ranking next in causes of cancer deaths are prostate and breast cancers followed closely by colorectal cancers (cancers of the colon and rectum).

Cancers among youngsters age 14 or under are rare. They account for about 9,500 new cases and 1,585 deaths each year. About one-third of the deaths are from leukemia.

Cancer incidence and death rates vary from nation to nation. For example, 83% of new liver cancer cases occur in developing countries. Liver cancer is the sixth most common type of cancer worldwide, the eighteenth most common in the United States.

Cancer incidence and death rates also vary geographically within a country. For instance, incidence is significantly higher in Kentucky than in Arizona. In this particular example, much of the difference is due to a markedly higher incidence of lung cancer in Kentucky. In Canada, cancer incidence and mortality rates are higher in eastern provinces and lower in western provinces.

The good news is that thanks to earlier detection and improved treatment, an increasing percentage of people diagnosed with cancer are surviving their illness. For example, death rates among children have declined about 49% since 1975.

Noticeable symptoms: Many changes occur with cancer. Cancers often form lumps or sores that can be felt or seen. Bleeding is a common symptom, as is unexplained pain. There may be otherwise unexplained symptoms of weight loss, nausea, or changes in bowel movements or stools. Sometimes persistent flulike symptoms occur as the immune system attempts to fight the disease. ***When in doubt, consult a physician.***

Often, cancer is detected not as a result of noticeable symptoms but through tests conducted during cancer-related checkups. Such tests include mammography to look for breast cancer, sigmoidoscopy to screen for colon cancer, the Pap smear to look for cervical cancer, and a blood test to look for abnormally high levels of prostate-specific antigen (PSA) for prostate cancer.

Diagnosis: Although a physician can often recognize cancer from experience or from viewing a sore, a sonogram, or an x-ray image, the main proof comes from *biopsy*, the direct examination of cells by a trained specialist called a *pathologist* (paa-THOL-uh-jihst). Cells removed from a lump (tumor), or in some cases from blood or other tissue, are examined under a microscope for characteristic changes. Depending on the location of the possible cancer, a tissue sample for a biopsy may be taken in a physician's office with little discomfort; however, the biopsy may require surgery in a hospital setting.

Stages and progress: Doctors use a process called staging to describe a cancer at the time it is diagnosed. Several different staging systems are in use, with one of the most common consisting of four stages labeled I through IV. Stage I is the earliest; the tumor is small, local, and comparatively easy to treat. Stage IV is the most advanced; the tumor is large and has metastasized, or spread, to distant parts of the body. With many cancer sites throughout the body, the disease becomes much more difficult to treat.

CANCER'S WARNING SIGNS

C hange in bowel or bladder habits

A sore that does not heal

U nusual bleeding or discharge

T hickening or lump in breast or elsewhere

I ndigestion or difficulty swallowing

O bvious change in a wart or mole

N agging cough or hoarseness

"Cure" in cancer is difficult to establish. Generally, physicians consider a five-year period free of symptoms as a cure. Many cancer patients, however, survive five years even while continuing to undergo treatment for the disease.

Survival rates vary greatly according to the type of cancer and the stage at which it is detected and treated. Two types of cancer can be used as examples. For lung cancer, only about 15% of patients are alive five years after diagnosis. Among those diagnosed with Stage I lung cancer, almost 50% are alive, but among those with Stage IV, only about 2% are alive. Prognosis is much better for women with breast cancer: The overall five-year survival rate is about 88%, ranging from about 98% for Stage I patients down to about 26% for those with Stage IV. Part of the difference between the survival rates of lung and breast cancer is ease of detection. Lung cancer usually has no noticeable symptoms in its early stages and so is not detected until it has advanced; breast cancer is easier to detect, either through self-examination or with mammography.

Treatment options: From ancient times medical practitioners have treated cancers by removing tumors with surgery. This approach is usually successful if the cancer has not metastasized or taken over an organ needed for life. In many cases, however, modern treatment also includes radiation, chemicals, or bone-marrow transplants. Exactly what treatment a specific patient receives depends on many factors, including the stage of the cancer, its location, and the person's overall health.

Surgery in the past often involved removal of large body parts and organs. Today surgeons try to remove the minimum necessary to get rid of the disease. For example, in the past, treatment of breast cancer involved removing the entire breast. Today, early-stage breast cancer is often treated with a procedure called a lumpectomy, in which only the tumor and a surrounding ring of normal tissue is removed.

About half of all cancer patients undergo radiation therapy, which uses ionizing radiation from x-rays or radioactive materials such as cobalt-60. The radiation kills rapidly dividing cancer cells somewhat faster than it does normal cells. A patient may receive treatments prior to surgery to shrink a tumor, or after surgery, to kill any cancerous cells remaining in the area. The radiation may be applied from without—for instance, aiming a beam of radiation at the specific location on a breast where a tumor was removed. Or the radioactive material may be surgically implanted, an alternative sometimes used to treat prostate cancer.

Advances in chemical therapy or *chemotherapy* (kee-moh-THEHR-uh-pee) have been largely responsible for the improved cure rates of recent years. Unlike surgery and radiation, which are local therapies, chemotherapy affects the entire body. The chemicals are carried by the blood, reaching cancerous cells that may have detached from the original tumor and lodged elsewhere. Usually a patient receives a "cocktail" of drugs that attack rapidly dividing cells; some drugs prevent cell division or growth, some interfere with DNA replication, and so on.

Chemotherapy and radiation can destroy blood-forming stem cells (cells at the earlier stage of development) found in the bone marrow. To restore the bone marrow's ability to produce blood cells, a patient may receive a transplant of bone marrow or a blood stem cell transplant. The procedure is most often used in the treatment of leukemia and lymphoma. Like radiation and chemotherapy, transplants are stressful and can have a variety of unpleasant side effects.

During and after treatment, membership in support groups can provide patients and their families with emotional and practical assistance. At group meetings, people share their feelings, learn the latest information on treatments, and discuss ways to cope with their illness. Some groups have broad memberships while others are devoted to a specific cancer or age group.

Prevention and risk factors: Although cancer results from inherited or acquired errors in DNA, it is not usually a purely hereditary disease. Even when genetic heritage predisposes a person to cancer, additional DNA mutations are usually required to initiate production of a tumor. Many factors may play a role in damaging DNA. Often the body can repair the damage, but over the years mutations build up. Thus, simple aging increases the likelihood that a person will develop cancer.

A variety of environmental factors have been implicated in cancer. Researchers have proved that some of these definitely increase risk; for others the links are not proven. By modifying lifestyle and behavior, however, individuals can prevent at least some forms of cancer.

Did You Know?

It's a myth that a teenager's behavior doesn't affect the chance of getting cancer later in life. Teens who smoke cigarettes, don't get enough exercise, or spend lots of time baking in the sun increase their risk of developing cancer years later. Even if people eventually drop such bad habits the harmful effects don't disappear, though they are greatly diminished.

12-Step meeting

Side effects of cancer treatment

Treatment for cancer can have many unpleasant side effects, resulting from damage to normal cells. These side effects can adversely affect a patient's life, particularly because treatment is often extended over months or years. The doctor can tell a patient what side effects to expect, for these vary according to the treatment the patient undergoes. A common side effect of chemotherapy is hair loss—often total during therapy, though complete regrowth usually occurs when treatment is ended. Nausea and vomiting used to be common side effects of chemotherapy but new antinausea drugs have greatly reduced these problems. Fatigue, pain, anemia, nerve damage, swelling due to closure of lymph passages, and blood-clotting problems may result from chemotherapy. Fatigue, nausea, and low blood cell counts are possible side effects of radiation therapy.

Don't smoke

Avoid alcohol

Food and physical activity: Research suggests that one-third of cancer deaths each year are due to diet and lack of physical exercise. A few chemicals found in food, such as those from aflatoxin molds that infect grains and peanuts, have been proven to cause cancer. Hundreds of other chemicals in food are suspected to be cancer promoters. In contrast, many people believe that ingesting more of certain chemicals, such as particular vitamins, can prevent cancer. But the relation between nutrition and cancer is extremely complex, and medical experts advise that the best plan is to eat a healthy, well-balanced diet. Such a diet is rich in fruits, vegetables, and whole-grain foods; it limits consumption of red meat, fats, and processed foods.

Maintaining a healthy weight is critical. Being overweight or obese has been linked to cancers of the breast, liver, pancreas, kidney, colon, and rectum. Moderate, daily exercise should play a central role in weight control and in maintaining a healthy body.

Tobacco and alcohol: The main known cause of preventable cancer is the use of tobacco, which greatly increases the risk of many kinds of cancer. Heavy drinking of alcoholic beverages is known to induce cancer, particularly of the mouth, esophagus, pancreas, and liver.

Water: Chlorinated water raises the risk of rectal and bladder cancers. However, the risks of infection from untreated water are far greater than the added cancer burden. And, of course, drinking plentiful amounts of water is critical to good general health.

Sex and reproduction: Some cancers are associated with the act of sex; for example, genital warts spread sexually can become malignant. Women who have had children have a lower risk of ovarian cancer, but the reason is unknown.

Occupation: The role of occupational exposure to chemicals in developing cancer has been difficult to prove except in the most clear-cut instances, such as asbestos-caused lung cancer. Farm workers have higher than average cancer rates, and pesticides are suspected. Chemicals used in such industries as manufacturing of computer chips are suspected as well. Dioxins, chemicals produced as byproducts of certain manufacturing processes and found in ash from garbage incineration, have been shown to cause cancer in animals; there is some evidence linking them to cancer in humans. Other chemicals considered possible human carcinogens based on animal studies include formaldehyde, chloroform, and polychlorinated biphenyls (PCBs).

Radiation: Exposure to the ultraviolet radiation in sunlight is the major cause of skin cancer, including deadly melanoma. Avoiding the sun in midday, when ultraviolet exposure is most intense, and regular use of good sunscreens help reduce risk.

Stay out of sun

Radiation from x-rays or radioactive elements is so powerful a cause of cancer that most workers with heavy exposure to radiation develop the disease. Wearing special protective clothing and other steps reduce the risk.

Radon is a colorless, odorless radioactive gas that escapes from granite and other rocks. It may enter people's homes through the basement. It can contribute to lung cancer unless air in affected basements is exchanged with outside air on a regular basis.

Electromagnetic fields, such as those from high-voltage, long-distance transmission lines, are suspected by some people of causing cancer. So, too, is the radiation emitted by cell phones. No clear connection between these types of radiation and cancer has been identified, however.

Germs: Infection is known to cause some types of cancer and is suspected in others. Liver cancer can be induced by the hepatitis B virus; a vaccine is available that prevents the original disease and thus the risk of cancer. The bacterium *Helicobacter pylori,* the chief cause of stomach and duodenal ulcers, is implicated in stomach cancer; treating the infection with antibiotics is a first line of cancer prevention.

Candidiasis

(KAAN-dih-DIY-uh-sihs)

DISEASE

TYPE: FUNGAL INFECTION

See also
Fungus diseases

Candidiasis is mainly a fungal infection of the skin and mucous membranes. Typical sites include the mouth and throat (*thrush*) and the female vagina (*vaginal yeast infection*). Much less common is *invasive candidiasis,* in which the infection enters the bloodstream, threatening damage to the liver, kidneys, or other internal organs.

Cause: Candidiasis is caused by a single-celled yeast called *Candida.* The yeast cells are ubiquitous—present everywhere—and ordinarily the body keeps their numbers under control. They cannot, for example, reproduce well on dry skin. On the moist mucous membranes bacteria keep them in check. The immune system also attacks them.

Under certain circumstances, however, the yeast organisms may reproduce out of control. When babies aren't kept dry between diaper changes, colonies grow on the moist skin. When antibiotics are used to fight bacterial infections, they may also kill off the useful bacteria on the mucous membranes. Also, any disorder that weakens the immune system reduces protection against the yeast.

Incidence: Because the yeast is naturally widespread, infections are very common.

Noticeable symptoms: The skin or mucous membranes are irritated by the spreading yeast colonies and become inflamed—red, itchy, and sore. If the infection occurs in the mouth, milky white patches of the yeast may be visible. A vaginal infection may produce a thick, whitish discharge. Itching in moist folds of the body, such as between the scrotum and thigh in men, is another symptom.

Diagnosis: Samples of the yeast cells can be identified under a microscope. If *Candida* invades the esophagus, it is diagnosed using an endoscope, a tube passed down the throat.

Treatment options: Candidiasis is successfully treated with antifungal medicines, either applied *topically* (on the surface) or taken internally.

Risk factors: People who have to undergo extended treatment with antibiotics or corticosteroids are at higher than usual risk. So are pregnant women and diabetics; men with diabetes may develop a *Candida* infection under the foreskin of the penis. People with damaged immune systems (such as those with AIDS or those receiving cancer treatment) are especially susceptible.

Canker

DISEASE

TYPE: UNKNOWN

See also
Cold sore

A small sore in the mouth that develops rapidly but usually heals without treatment may be a canker, or *aphthous* (AAF-thuhs) *ulcer*. Cankers resemble cold sores; however, unlike cold sores, cankers are not contagious.

Cause: Cankers are very common, but their cause is unknown. A number of infectious agents, including viruses and bacteria, have been implicated. There is some evidence that cankers are an autoimmune disorder related to a reaction to one's own immune system. Also, heredity may be involved, with some people predisposed to developing cankers. Various factors seem to trigger outbreaks, including stress, food allergies, nutritional deficiencies, and hormone changes related to menstruation.

Noticeable symptoms: Cankers may occur singly or in clusters. They develop in the fleshy lining of the mouth and on the tongue. A canker typically is less than 0.08 inch in diameter, but may be ten times that size. It resembles a tiny crater, having a yellow or whitish gray center enclosed within a narrow red ring. For about a week the canker stings, especially when one eats or drinks. Then, as the sore begins to heal, the pain lessens. Most cankers heal within two weeks.

Treatment options: Cankers usually heal by themselves. Pain can be relieved by rinsing the mouth several times a day with an antiseptic mouthwash or warm salt water. Both prescription and nonprescription ointments are available to numb the pain; these can be applied to the canker with a cotton swab. If cankers recur frequently or if sores do not heal within three weeks, see a doctor. He or she will examine the mouth for punctures or other injuries. The doctor may recommend blood tests or a biopsy of a sore to determine if there is an underlying cause that requires attention.

Capillaries

(KAAP-uh-LEHR-eez)

The capillaries are tiny blood vessels that deliver fresh blood directly to cells and that remove waste products from the cells. If you think of the circulatory system as being to the body as a water supply and sewers are to a city, then the capillaries are the plumbing pipes in individual kitchens and bathrooms.

Size: The walls of capillaries are only one cell thick, and the cells are flattened like pizzas. A molecule can easily pass from one side of such a cell to the other, conducted through the cell membranes by special protein complexes that project through the membranes and provide passageways.

The smallest capillaries are only three-thousandths of an inch in diameter. Red blood cells, which collect and release oxygen, must pass through the tubes in single file.

Role: Oxygen from blood escapes through capillary walls into body tissues, replaced in the blood by carbon dioxide from the tissues. Water molecules can also penetrate to some degree, along with small molecules dissolved in the blood fluid. As a result, the space around cells is bathed in fluid. Blood pressure maintains a balance between this fluid and the plasma in the capillaries, but there is nearly three times as much fluid outside the circulatory system as in blood. Excess fluid is carried away by the lymphatic system.

The fluid that escapes from the capillaries provides a route for the cells of the immune system to travel to other body cells. Thus, when bacteria or viruses invade cells, the immune system can bring up its army and attack. White blood cells, such as phagocytes and other leukocytes, pass through capillaries' thin walls. (Red blood cells have no passage out of the circulatory system in a healthy body.)

Conditions that affect the capillaries: In hemorrhagic fevers capillaries break and cause bleeding. The red nose of the chronic alcohol abuser stems from a thinning of the capillaries caused by excessive drinking. In a condition called *diabetic retinopathy* (REHT-uhn-AHP-uh-thee) capillaries in the retina may break. This can lead to visual impairment or blindness if not controlled.

Did You Know?
Armed with a new invention, the compound microscope, 17th-century Italian anatomist Marcello Malpighi discovered blood capillaries. Malpighi also was the first person to study fingerprints scientifically.

Carbuncle	*See* **Boils**
Cardiac	*See* **Heart; Heart attack; Heart failure**

Cardiac muscle

The regular beat of the heart about once a second or faster continues throughout a person's life, amounting to more than 2 billion contractions. This heartbeat is among the remarkable feats of the body. A special kind of muscle is needed to accomplish this feat.

Size and location: The muscle tissue of the heart is a special type called cardiac muscle. Its fibers are striped, resembling skeletal muscle. But the stripes in cardiac muscle are bridges that connect one fiber to the next. These bridges account for the involuntary way the heart works, resembling smooth muscle in operating with no conscious control. However, cardiac muscle continues to beat with no outside control, conscious or unconscious. The regular muscle contractions go on even if a section of the heart is removed and kept alive for a time. The bridges are the key to this because they keep adjacent muscle cells beating together.

Role: The heart is one of the main mechanical parts of the body, with the cardiac muscle doing the work of pumping blood through the circulatory system.

Conditions that affect cardiac muscle: Because of its constant activity cardiac muscle requires a steady supply of oxygen to burn glucose for energy. Angina is pain registered by heart muscle that is receiving too little oxygen. Nitroglycerin used to relieve angina apparently works by increasing the supply of the compound nitric oxide in heart muscle, which promotes relaxation. More serious problems arise when oxygen is cut off for even a short time by a blood clot, perhaps the most common type of heart attack.

Inflammation of the heart muscle, or myocarditis (MIY-oh-kahr-DIY-tis), can result from any of several infectious diseases, but especially as a side effect of diphtheria or AIDS. It can also be induced by radiation and cocaine abuse as well as sometimes being a side effect of prescription drugs.

The general name for damage to cardiac muscle is *cardiomyopathy* (KAHR-dee-oh-miy-OP-uh-thee). There are several kinds of damage. Active alcoholism damages heart muscle either as a direct effect of alcohol abuse or through B-vitamin deficiency. Vitamin B_1 deficiency by itself can also cause cardiomyopathy. High blood pressure may affect heart muscle as well. Furthermore, in some individuals the cardiac muscle degenerates for reasons that are unknown at the present time.

An enlarged heart, called *cardiac hypertrophy,* can develop when cardiac muscle increases in bulk because pumping is insufficient. The enlarged heart can produce pressure on nearby organs such as the lungs and often does not succeed in better pumping despite its increased size.

Cardiomyopathy	*See* **Cardiac muscle; Heart failure**
Caries, dental	*See* **Tooth decay**

Carpal tunnel syndrome

INJURY

TYPE: MECHANICAL

See also
Cartilage
Ligaments
Nerves
Tennis elbow and related problems

The median nerve, which supplies sensation to the thumb and adjacent fingers, reaches the hand through a canal called the carpal tunnel. The tunnel is formed by bones called carpals at the base of the palm and the ligament that covers them. Tendons and the median nerve pass through this narrow space. Pressure can compress the nerve, reducing its ability to carry signals to and from the hand. The result is pain and numbness, a condition called carpal tunnel syndrome.

Cause: The problem is not with the nerve but with its surroundings. Sometimes the cause is hereditary: The person is born with a narrow carpal tunnel. More often, compression appears to result from trauma, such as a wrist sprain or fracture. Excess weight, overactivity of the pituitary gland, thyroid disease, diabetes, and rheumatoid arthritis have been linked to carpal tunnel syndrome. Women who experience fluid retention during pregnancy or menopause also are at risk.

Carpal tunnel syndrome is often confused with *repetitive stress syndrome.* This disorder occurs when a person performs the

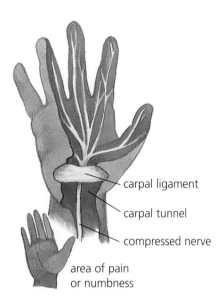

carpal ligament

carpal tunnel

compressed nerve

area of pain
or numbness

Carpal tunnel syndrome occurs
when swelling in the tunnel harms
the nerve that passes through it.

same action over and over, putting too much stress on a joint. For example, heavy computer use, with improper wrist positions, may cause repetitive stress syndrome. Food-service workers who spend long hours chopping and cutting, athletes in certain sports, people who do needlework or other crafts involving the fingers and wrists, and amateur and professional musicians also have an increased risk of this type of repetitive stress syndrome.

Incidence: Carpal tunnel syndrome affects an estimated 2 to 3% of the population. Women are two to three times as likely as men to have the condition, possibly because their carpal tunnel tends to be smaller than that of men. The syndrome almost always occurs in adults, and incidence increases with age. Surgery to reduce pressure on the median nerve is very common in the United States, with more than 200,000 procedures performed annually.

Noticeable symptoms: Numbness or tingling in the hands, especially at night, is a major symptom. The numbness or tingling is in all but the little finger because that finger receives signals from a different nerve, one that does not pass through the carpal tunnel. Hands may also become "clumsy" as a loss of strength develops, making it more difficult to grasp and hold objects between the thumb and fingers, to perform delicate tasks such as buttoning buttons, or to turn objects such as door handles. Some people feel pain in their hands, wrists, and sometimes arms or shoulders. The hands may also seem cold. At first the person may experience only occasional mild or moderate discomfort, but over time symptoms may become constant and increasingly severe.

Diagnosis: A healthcare worker will ask you to bend back your hand to test the flexibility of the wrist. You may squeeze a device that measures strength of the hands and fingers. Another test involves holding the hands together as if praying, but upside down; after a few moments the healthcare worker will ask about numbness or tingling. He or she will also tap the hands and arms lightly and ask about tingling sensations; the diagnostician may also ask which fingers are affected by tingling and numbness. These tests will determine whether the problem is caused by carpal tunnel syndrome and will also show the seriousness of any damage.

In some cases the healthcare worker may do a nerve conduction study, or electromyography (ih-LEHK-troh-miy-AHG-ruh-fee). For this test he or she inserts needles at several places on the arm, then runs very low voltage electricity through the needles. The test shows the location of any nerve damage.

Treatment options: Treatment for carpal tunnel syndrome should begin as early as possible to limit the amount of damage. Any underlying causes, such as diabetes or rheumatoid arthritis, will be treated first. The patient will be advised to rest the affected hand and wrist, giving up any activities that strain these structures and worsen symptoms. Moist heat and cold packs often reduce swelling and help ease pain.

Oral anti-inflammatory drugs such as ibuprofen, naproxen, or aspirin may be prescribed to relieve pain and reduce inflammation. If these are not sufficiently effective, corticosteroids, such as cortisone, may be prescribed. However, these drugs can cause unwanted side effects.

The doctor may recommend wearing a splint on the wrist to keep the hand and wrist straight and reduce tingling and numbness. If after six months or so these and other measures are not sufficiently effective, surgery may be necessary. This involves cutting the carpal ligament to enlarge the carpal tunnel. The surgery is done under local anesthesia and usually does not require an overnight stay in a hospital.

Following surgery, the patient may experience pain. He or she may be sent to a licensed physical therapist to learn stretching and strengthening exercises. An occupational therapist can help the patient build skills to better deal with permanent physical impairments. Some patients have found alternative therapies such as acupuncture, chiropractic, and yoga to be helpful in reducing pain and improving hand-and-wrist strength.

Prevention: Other than dealing with underlying causes such as diabetes, there are no strategies known to prevent carpal tunnel syndrome. However, certain steps can help avoid hand-and-wrist ailments, including repetitive stress injuries: (1) Learn how to do repetitive tasks in ways that will not strain the hands, wrists, and arms. (2) Take frequent breaks when doing repetitive tasks. (3) Use only as much force as is absolutely necessary to get a job done; for example, instead of hitting computer keys, touch them softly. (4) Do stretching exercises to keep muscles flexible before beginning and after finishing a task. If you spend an hour or more at a task, such as using equipment that vibrates, take breaks every half hour and do stretching exercises.

Repetitive stress injuries can be caused by keyboarding or other tasks that use the same motions over and over. Stopping the repetitive motions from time to time—say every hour or so—and stretching the muscles involved helps prevent this kind of injury. For keyboarding, a good stretching break includes making a fist and then spreading the fingers, which should be repeated several times, relaxing the hands before going back to the keyboard. Similar stretching exercises should be used before starting keyboarding.

Cartilage

BODY SYSTEM

Cartilage is a flexible substance that precedes bone development in children and that is found in adults at *joints,* places where bones meet, as well as in organs that combine stiffness with flexibility.

Although cartilage is found in all vertebrates, such as bony fish, amphibians, reptiles, birds, and mammals, it is especially prominent in sharks and rays, which have skeletons of cartilage instead of bone.

Size, role, and location: Most cartilage in an adult covers joints. It also forms a strengthening framework in the nose and exterior ears; in flexible tubes such as the bronchi, esophagus, and trachea; and in the larynx. Considerable cartilage occurs as part of the spinal column and attached to the ribs.

There are three main types of cartilage: white, yellow, and fibrous. All three consist of cells and cell products such as fibers made from a substance called *collagen* (KOL-uh-juhn), but cartilage does not contain blood vessels or nerves. Some people refer only to the fibers and the matrix the fibers are in as cartilage. A membrane around each structure made from cartilage contains blood vessels as well as stem cells that migrate into the cartilage to become cartilage-producing cells.

Conditions that affect cartilage: Joint diseases, such as rheumatoid arthritis or osteoarthritis, are diseases of cartilage more than of bone or ligament, although other tissues are involved. Many autoimmune diseases attack connective tissue, especially collagen, and therefore are diseases of cartilage.

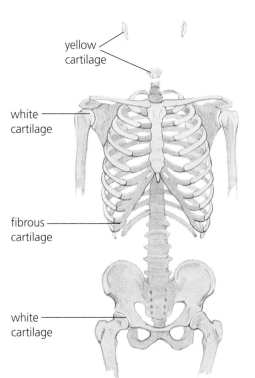

yellow cartilage

white cartilage

fibrous cartilage

white cartilage

Three kinds of cartilage
Yellow cartilage is in the larynx and ears. Fibrous cartilage is in the spinal column and attached to ribs. White cartilage is found at certain movable joints.

Conditions that affect the structure of the nose are basically disorders of cartilage. Some genetic disorders that affect cartilage result in extreme height or in short stature.

Cartilage that is damaged is slow to heal. It can sometimes break, with a piece lodging in a part of the joint where it does not belong. In that case the fragment needs to be surgically removed.

The cartilage that attaches the ribs to the *sternum* can become painfully inflamed. The exact cause of this condition is not known, but it usually returns to normal after a short time. A rare cancer can occur in cartilage, but it is slow growing and usually can be successfully removed with surgery.

Cataract
(KAAT-uh-raakt)

DISEASE

TYPE: MECHANICAL

See also
Allergies
Down syndrome
Eyes and vision
Rubella ("German" measles)
Viruses and disease

On the Internet
ST. LUKE'S CATARACT
& LASER INSTITUTE
www.stlukeseye.com/Conditions/
Cataracts.asp

In young people the lens of the eye is normally transparent. For a variety of reasons this transparency may decrease over time. The lens takes on a degree of clouding, or opacity, that causes increasingly blurry vision. This condition is known as a cataract.

Cause: There are many different causes of cataracts. The so-called senile cataract, by far the most common, is caused by long-term exposure to the ultraviolet portion of sunlight. Over time the higher energy light waves "cook" protein fibers in the lens. Just as boiling causes the liquid albumin of an egg to turn to solid white, so light causes the fibers to exude a yellow-brown pigment that clouds vision. This rarely occurs in persons less than 50 years of age.

Less frequent causes of cataracts are poor nutrition, a history of allergic skin reactions, direct injury to the eye, severe diabetes, smoking, contact with certain poisons, and the taking of some steroid drugs.

A condition known as *congenital* (present at birth) *cataract* occurs rarely in infants. Congenital cataracts may occur as the result of a pregnant woman's becoming infected with a viral disease, especially rubella (German measles). Congenital cataracts may also occur as a side effect of certain genetic conditions such as Down syndrome.

Incidence: Almost everyone over 65 has some degree of senile cataract in one or both eyes, though people who spend a great deal of time in sunlight may experience problems sooner. More than 5.5 million Americans have some vision loss from cataract, and 400,000 new cases are diagnosed annually in the United States. It is estimated that, worldwide, 20% of all persons over 65 develop cataract. This makes cataract the leading cause of blindness around the world, with perhaps 5 million new cases each year, nearly all of them in less developed nations.

Noticeable symptoms: All cataracts are painless. Except in the case of congenital cataract, the condition usually becomes apparent only with age. The first signs may come in the form of reduced sensitivity to different colors and in problems with glare, particularly associated with night driving. Farsighted people may be pleasantly surprised to find that they can read without glasses, a temporary phenomenon sometimes called "second sight." Eventually, however, some degree of blurring usually occurs, or perhaps double vision or other distortions.

Diagnosis: Using a handheld ophthalmoscope (of-THAAL-muh-SKOHP) (lighted device for observing the interior of the eye), a physician can track the size, location, and severity of a cataract almost from the beginning. As the condition progresses, clouding may become observable even without instruments, appearing as a dull whitish area in the center of the eye. It was once common practice to delay surgical treatment until the cataract "ripened" to the point that vision was greatly impaired. But today, with cataract surgery an outstanding success in 95% of cases, the usual practice is to operate whenever the patient begins to experience a degree of loss that interferes with normal activities.

Treatment options: Short of surgical removal of the clouded lens, there is no effective way to reverse the vision changes related to cataracts. But stronger prescription glasses or contact lenses, as well as improved lighting in work areas, can often postpone treatment.

Eventually, however, the only reasonable course of treatment for otherwise healthy individuals is surgical removal of the clouded lens and replacement of the lens with another means of focusing—usually a plastic lens sewn into the eye called an *intraocular* (IHN-truh-OK-yuh-luhr) *implant*. The replacement lens is permanently implanted in the space previously occupied by the natural lens. Such cataract surgery is the most frequently performed of all operations in persons over 65.

The operation itself typically takes about an hour and is performed in a hospital or ophthalmic clinic on an outpatient basis. In the most frequently used procedure the patient is given local or general anesthesia, after which the surgeon makes a small half-moon incision around the upper edge of the cornea, using a fine diamond-tipped instrument. After a small amount of clear gel is injected into the space surrounding the clouded lens, the lens itself is emulsified by ultrasound waves or a laser and vacuumed away. Finally, the artificial implant is slipped in place. The incision is self-sealing, and no stitches are needed. Upon waking, the patient is given antibiotics and sent home. Full recovery is almost immediate though patients may be instructed to avoid stooping or strenuous activity for several days.

In a minority of patients for whom intraocular implants are not recommended, prescription glasses or contact lenses are alternatives.

Stay out of sun

Don't smoke

Prevention and risk factors: Exposure to sunlight is the main risk factor; smoking tobacco is another. Diabetes doubles the risk and also lowers the age at which cataracts occur. Men who are obese also have a higher risk, especially taller men and those with a waist-to-hip ratio greater than one.

To slow the development of cataract, wear ultraviolet-screening sunglasses outdoors or ultraviolet-screening coatings on prescription glasses, especially when at higher altitudes. A diet high in antioxidants, such as vitamins A, C, or E, also slows the development of cataracts. People with diabetes can slow the progress of cataracts by proper monitoring and control of their blood sugar. And, of course, stop smoking.

Cat-scratch fever

DISEASE

TYPE: INFECTIOUS
(BACTERIAL)

Many people who are scratched by healthy cats develop cat-scratch fever, a minor local inflammation followed by fever.

Cause: Cat-scratch fever is caused almost exclusively by a small rod-shaped bacterium, *Bartonella henselae*. Almost all cases follow contact with cats and typically involve cat scratches or bites —rarely dog scratches or bites. Cat fleas also may spread the disease when they bite humans.

Incidence: Cat-scratch fever is a common disease all over the

On the Internet
CENTERS FOR DISEASE CONTROL
AND PREVENTION (CDC)
www.cdc.gov/healthypets/
diseases/catscratch.htm

Did You Know?
The National Center for
Infectious Diseases estimates
that 25% to 41% of America's
cat population carry the
bacteria that cause cat-scratch
fever.

world, though rare in the United States. Most cases occur in children under the age of 17, with the majority in children under the age of 12. AIDS patients and other people with compromised immune systems are most at risk for becoming seriously ill from cat-scratch fever.

Noticeable symptoms: Within three to ten days after being infected, a small, pus-filled lesion develops at the site of the scratch or other wound. As nearby lymph nodes become infected—within two weeks—they become enlarged and tender. This stage is accompanied by fever, headache, fatigue, and lack of appetite. The symptoms usually persist for two to four months, after which most people recover completely.

Diagnosis: A doctor will suspect cat-scratch fever if a patient has recently been scratched by a cat and has inflamed lymph nodes. The doctor may perform a skin test; if the skin reacts positively to a substance called cat-scratch antigen, the diagnosis is confirmed. Sometimes diagnosis includes a biopsy of an affected lymph node—taking a sample of cells from the node—to look for bacteria.

Treatment options: In many cases no treatment is necessary: Sometimes a doctor prescribes an antibiotic.

Celiac disease

(SEE-lee-AAK)

DISEASE

TYPE: GENETIC;
     AUTOIMMUNE

Celiac disease (often called sprue) is a partly genetic, partly autoimmune, disorder of the digestive organs, which varies widely in its severity and timing. A tropical infection with similar symptoms is also known as sprue, or tropical sprue.

Cause: The immediate cause is an abnormal sensitivity to the proteins, together known as gluten (GLOOT-n), contained in wheat, rye, barley, and probably oats, but *not* rice or maize (corn).

Celiac disease seems to be at least partly genetic—the disease is strongly familial. More than one gene may be involved, and environmental factors may also play a role. The symptoms of celiac disease stem from the immune system attacking part of the nutrient-absorbing apparatus of the small intestine, so it is classed as an autoimmune disease. The lining of the small intestine becomes damaged, hindering its normal ability to absorb fats and other nutrients from food.

Incidence: Celiac disease is quite common in the United States and Canada. About 1 in 133 persons has the disease, but most have not been diagnosed. This means that more than 2 million Americans and about 250,000 Canadians have the disorder.

Noticeable symptoms: Symptoms may occur when an infant first starts eating solid food, but they may be delayed for years. The most evident symptom is persistent diarrhea. It may be accompanied or followed by signs of malnutrition or anemia. In adults, one indication is unexplained weight loss. Infants may show failure to thrive and children may develop with short stature.

Since nutrients pass unabsorbed into the large intestine, they may provoke gas, cramps, and fatty diarrhea. Another consequence may be malnutrition, leading to retarded growth and to vitamin and mineral deficiency disorders such as iron-deficiency anemia. If identified and treated promptly, celiac disease need not have any lasting negative effects. However, untreated celiac disease can lead to anemia, osteoporosis, miscarriage, seizures, or cancers of the intestinal tract.

Diagnosis: A series of blood tests, x-rays, and a biopsy of the intestinal lining may be required. A blood test for antibodies to gluten is helpful, but a biopsy showing characteristic damage to the small intestine is most definitive.

Treatment options: All grain products except rice and maize and any foods containing gluten, often as thickeners or extenders, must be completely removed from the diet.

Cerebral palsy

(SEHR-uh-bruhl PAWL-zee)

DISORDER

TYPE: DEVELOPMENTAL

Cerebral palsy is a group of disorders that result from damage to particular areas of the brain—the areas that control movement. The parts of the body most impaired are those that must move freely to function, such as the arms and legs and the tongue and other organs involved in speech.

Types: There are several forms of the disease.

Spastic: This is by far the most common form and also the one that varies most widely in severity. The muscles, particularly in the arms and legs, are abnormally contracted, or stiff, and subject to tremors.

Although a child may have many of the problems associated with cerebral palsy, many learn as they grow to cope with their disabilities and are able to attend school, hold jobs, and lead lives that are normal in most ways.

- developmental disabilities
- impaired vision
- hearing loss
- speech difficulties
- muscle spasticity
- paralysis

On the Internet
NATIONAL INSTITUTE OF NEUROLOGICAL DISEASES AND STROKE
www.ninds.nih.gov/disorders/cerebral_palsy/cerebral_palsy.htm

The most typical symptom is difficulty in walking. Persistently contracted thigh muscles may cause the knees and feet to turn, or *scissor*, inward. Stiff calf muscles may cause *toe walking*. Mildly affected children may display only slight clumsiness in their movements. Others, however, are unable to manage even the simplest voluntary motions.

Severe spasticity may prevent the muscles from stretching and lengthening as the bones grow. The muscles may become permanently shortened and stiffened, to become *contractures*.

Athetoid (AATH-uh-toid), or *dyskinetic:* Typical symptoms are spontaneous, involuntary movements, such as jerks or writhing. Those affected have trouble keeping their bodies stable, whether standing or sitting. The involuntary movements also make walking and speech difficult.

Ataxic: This form weakens the sense of balance, the perception of depth and distance, and the ability to reach objects accurately or to identify them by touch. Walking is unsteady, and activities that require precise coordination, such as writing, may be impaired.

Mixed: Some of those affected have symptoms of more than one form of the disease. Such mixed cerebral palsy reflects damage in more than one area of the brain and is likely to be especially severe.

Other problems are associated with cerebral palsy as well, including loss of hearing, impaired vision, and difficulties with eating and speech. Many affected children have at least occasional problems with bowel control. Furthermore, cerebral palsy is often accompanied by other central nervous system disorders, such as developmental disability (mental retardation) and epilepsy.

Cause: It was once thought that most cerebral palsy is caused by asphyxia during birth, in which a baby is deprived of sufficient oxygen during a difficult or prolonged delivery. But evidence now suggests that most damage occurs during prenatal development, well before birth.

The risk of a child having cerebral palsy can be raised by a number of harmful factors during pregnancy, including maternal infections such as rubella ("German" measles) and conditions such as Rh incompatibility that cause jaundice in newborns. Premature birth, for whatever reason, also raises the risk of brain damage and subsequent cerebral palsy.

In early childhood brain damage may result from a severe infection such as meningitis or from a violent head injury.

Incidence: Cerebral palsy is among the more common defects of the nervous system. Estimates are that it occurs in nearly 10,000 Americans and Canadians each year. The average rate is about 2 per 1,000 live births.

About 50% of persons with cerebral palsy have the spastic type, about 20% the athetoid type, and about 10% the ataxic. The remaining 20% have mixed types.

Noticeable symptoms: Early signs are difficult to identify, especially if the disorder is mild. An affected child may be unusually slow in learning to walk or talk—but this occurs in many normal children as well. By age two or three, however, the characteristic impairments of movement and speech are usually unmistakable.

Treatment options: Cerebral palsy cannot be cured, but some of its harmful effects can be minimized. Team effort, including drug therapy, physical therapy, occupational therapy, speech therapy, orthopedic treatment, special education, and (in some cases) surgery, is often required. The goals are to minimize disability, to avoid secondary complications such as contractures, and to enable the affected person to live as normally as possible.

Cervical and uterine cancers

DISEASE

TYPE: CANCER

See also
Birth canal
Cancers
Reproductive system
STD (sexually transmitted diseases)
Uterus

On the Internet
UNIVERSITY OF VIRGINIA
HEALTH SYSTEM
www.healthsystem.virginia.edu/
uvahealth/adult_gyneonc/
uterine.cfm

Abnormal bleeding or discharge from a woman's vagina may indicate the presence of a cervical or uterine cancer. When caught early, before they have spread to other organs, these cancers can usually be cured with treatment.

Parts affected: The uterus is the organ in a woman's body where an embryo grows into a baby. The embryo attaches to the lining of the uterus, called the *endometrium* (EHN-doh-MEE-tree-uhm). At the time of birth the baby leaves its mother's body through the lower part of the uterus. This narrow opening of the uterus, which leads to the vagina, is the *cervix* (SUHR-vihks).

Cause: Various factors appear to increase a woman's susceptibility to cervical/uterine cancers.

Virtually all cases of cervical cancer are linked sexually to certain human papillomaviruses (HPV) that cause genital warts. In particular, a virus called HPV-16 is thought to cause about half of all cervical cancers, while HPV-18 causes another 10% to 20%. Consequently, women who began having sexual intercourse at an early age, have had many sexual partners, or have a history of genital warts are at increased risk of developing cervical cancer.

Nearly all uterine cancer arises in the endometrium; that form is also called *endometrial cancer*. Susceptibility is linked to the endometrium's exposure to estrogen, a hormone that stimulates cell division. The greater the cumulative exposure to estrogen, the greater the risk of uterine cancer. Thus uterine cancer usually occurs in older women either during or following menopause. Women who began menstruating early, began menopause late, or never had children are at higher risk. So too are women who take estrogen replacement therapy that consists only of estrogen (as opposed to estrogen plus progesterone). The drug tamoxifen, used to treat breast cancer, increases the risk slightly. Obesity, diabetes, and hypertension also are risk factors.

Incidence: Each year approximately 10,000 American women are diagnosed with invasive cervical cancer and 40,000 with uterine cancer. Incidence rates for cervical cancer are higher among Hispanic and African American women, but a higher percentage of women with European ancestry develop uterine cancer. About 10,500 deaths from cervical and uterine cancers occur annually.

Noticeable symptoms: Cervical and uterine cancers develop long before they produce detectable symptoms. The first symptom a woman is likely to notice is abnormal vaginal bleeding or watery discharge. If a cancer has spread to nearby tissues, it is said to be invasive. Symptoms of invasive cervical and uterine cancers may include fatigue, weight loss, backaches, leg pain, and difficult urination. *A woman who experiences any of these symptoms should see a doctor as soon as possible.*

Phone doctor

Diagnosis: The doctor will conduct a complete pelvic examination. A *Pap smear,* which scrapes tissue from the cervix, will be performed and checked for abnormal cells. The Pap smear can detect cells that will become cervical cancer even before cancer has started. Ultrasound may be used to look for causes of the woman's symptoms. If suspicious cells are detected, a *biopsy* will be performed. In this procedure a small amount of tissue is removed from the suspect area and examined under a microscope. A procedure called *dilation and curettage* (D&C) may be performed to obtain endometrial tissue for examination. If the biopsy or D&C confirms cancer, blood studies and other tests can help determine the stage of the disease.

Stages and progress: Knowing the stage of a cancer enables a physician to choose the most effective treatment. Staging describes the size of the tumor and whether it has spread to other organs. A widely used system assigns a stage of I, II, III, or IV. I is an early stage, with no indication that the cancer has spread beyond the cervix or uterus. IV is the most advanced stage, with the cancer having spread, or *metastasized,* to distant parts of the body. The more advanced the cancer, the more difficult it is to treat.

Treatment options: Early noninvasive cervical cancer may be removed surgically, using a scalpel or laser. Alternate treatments include destroying the cancerous cells by freezing them (cyrotherapy) or exposing them to intense heat (electrocoagulation). Invasive cervical cancer is treated by surgery, radiation, and perhaps chemotherapy.

Early uterine cancer is usually treated by surgery. Especially in patients who have children or with later stages of cervical or uterine cancer, complete removal of the uterus and cervix may be performed (a *hysterectomy*). Removal of all the female sex organs including the ovaries is called a *total hysterectomy*. If the cancer has spread beyond the uterus, radiation therapy typically follows surgery. Chemotherapy may also be used.

Regular, frequent medical checkups are recommended during the five years following treatment. Assuming no recurrence, annual checkups are recommended after the first five years.

Prevention: New vaccines for dangerous strains of human papillomaviruses can prevent about 95% of cases of cervical cancer. They are especially effective when administered to teenagers. Safe-sex practices also lower the risk of sexually transmitted diseases that may lead to cervical cancer. A woman should have a Pap smear and pelvic exam every year after age 18 or after becoming sexually active.

High levels of estrogen in the blood can promote uterine cancer. Oral contraceptives and a low-fat diet can reduce circulating estrogen.

Chest pain

SYMPTOM

See also
Angina
Bronchitis
Cancers
Embolism
Fractures, dislocations, sprains, and strains
Fungus diseases
GERD (gastroesophageal reflux disease)
Heart attack
Heartburn
Pleurisy
Pneumonia
Scleroderma
Shingles

Chest pain can range from a dull pressure or ache to a burning sensation or a severe squeezing or crushing feeling. Although people often connect chest pain to heart attack, there are a number of different injuries, disorders, and diseases that can also cause chest pain.

Parts affected: Chest pain may occur anywhere from the neck down to the bottom of the ribs. Most of the organs located in the chest can produce pain, but commonly pain originates in a muscle or in the esophagus, heart, or lungs. Inflammation of the lining of the chest, or pleurisy, is a cause of chest pain.

Related symptoms: Severe crushing pain that starts over the heart and moves up to the neck and shoulders may mean that the heart is not getting enough oxygen—a heart attack. A recurring pain in the chest may be angina, which is also caused by heart disease.

Pain caused by a heart problem is often accompanied by sweating, nausea, dizziness, or difficulty in breathing. Pale, blue, cold, or clammy skin is another sign. If the heart is deprived of sufficient oxygen for too long, a heart attack can induce loss of consciousness or be fatal.

Call ambulance

Coughing, shortness of breath, or an above normal temperature may accompany bronchitis, pneumonia, or other causes of chest pain. Pleurisy tends to produce severe pain on one side of the chest only. A sharp pain that appears from nowhere may be a lung clot (*pulmonary embolism*). **Contact an emergency medical service immediately since this condition may be fatal if not treated.** Another equally dangerous lung condition, spontaneously collapsed lung, is marked by milder chest pain that increases while inhaling.

Heartburn is typically accompanied by an acid taste in the mouth. The pain may increase in postures that push up the stomach or lower the esophagus.

A pain that appears only when moving the upper body, arms, or neck is usually caused by a pulled muscle.

Associations: Bronchitis or pneumonia may cause pain deep in the chest. Several diseases produced when a fungus invades the lungs also produce chest pain.

The burning in the chest due to heartburn is the result of stomach acid backing up into the esophagus, a condition more formally known as GERD (gastroesophageal reflux disease). The esophagus may also cause pain through spasms or incomplete emptying of food, called *achalasia* (AAK-uh-LAY-zhuh). Diseases such as scleroderma or cancer can also produce esophageal pain.

A burning feeling in the skin on one side of the chest may be due to a viral infection called shingles.

Prevention and possible actions: Stretching and other warm-ups can help prevent muscle pulls. A diet low in fat and cholesterol helps reduce heart problems. Small meals are less likely to cause heartburn.

Phone doctor

Pain with symptoms of heart attack, lung clot, or collapsed lung should receive immediate medical attention. *It is best not to ignore any type of chest pain. Consult a physician as to the cause.*

Relief of symptoms: Pain from bronchitis or pneumonia can be relieved with rest, use of a humidifier, and cough medicine. An antacid normally relieves heartburn, which is one way of distinguishing heartburn from heart attack, which is not relieved by antacids. Application of an ice pack will often ease the pain of a pulled muscle. Heart attack or severe lung problems must be treated by a physician.

Chicken pox

DISEASE

TYPE: INFECTIOUS (VIRAL)

See also
Blister
Itching
Rashes
Reye's syndrome
Shingles
Viruses and disease

On the Internet
KIDS HEALTH
kidshealth.org/parent/
infections/skin/chicken_pox.html

CENTERS FOR DISEASE CONTROL AND PREVENTION (CDC)
www.cdc.gov/nip/diseases/
varicella

Once, most children contracted chicken pox. While it usually involves a mild but unpleasant itchy rash and fever, this childhood disease often has serious consequences. Today, thanks to the introduction of an effective vaccine in 1995, chicken pox, also known as *varicella* (VEHR-ih-SEHL-uh), is becoming as rare as measles or mumps.

Cause: *Varicella zoster* is the virus that causes chicken pox. It is carried in saliva and mucus and can be spread when an infected person coughs or sneezes. After a person is infected with *Varicella*, the virus produces the symptoms known as chicken pox. Then it hides. The virus remains hidden in the body in nerves or in the brain. It remains dormant there for years. Later in life it may become active and cause shingles, a condition with pain in the infected nerve and a rash on the body or face.

Varicella zoster is in the herpes family of viruses. All the herpes viruses are able to hide from the immune system. They emerge and attack when the immune system has been weakened, often by stress.

Incidence: Chicken pox has been one of the most common viral infections of children around the world. Most children who have not been vaccinated become infected before the age of ten. Before the vaccine was introduced, about 4 million cases occurred in the United States each year, but it is estimated that this number has dropped to about 400,000 in recent years.

Noticeable symptoms: The most obvious symptom is a rash that starts on the body and scalp and spreads to the face, arms, and legs. A fever may also be present. The person with chicken pox may feel tired and generally ill.

Diagnosis: A doctor will want to examine the rash. Since rashes can have many different causes, it is best to have a doctor diagnose the disease in person instead of over the telephone. He or she may ask about contact with other children who have chicken pox or measles or other diseases that cause rashes. A blood sample will reveal a low white blood cell count.

Treatment options: Since chicken pox is caused by a virus, antibiotics or other medicines cannot knock it out. One has to depend on the immune system. Antiviral medications, such as acyclovir, can help reduce the severity of chicken pox, especially in individuals with faulty immune systems.

Avoid aspirin

A physician can prescribe lotions or creams to reduce the itchiness of the rash and to help dry it up. Antihistamines may also relieve some of the itchiness. Showers with a mild soap help prevent the sores from becoming infected with bacteria.

Pain-relieving medicine may be prescribed if blisters form in the mouth or close to the eyes. *Aspirin should never be taken to relieve chicken pox symptoms.* Sometimes when people with chicken pox take aspirin, they develop a condition called Reye's syndrome, which can be fatal. *Call the physician if symptoms such as excessive sleepiness or difficult breathing develop; these could signal Reye's syndrome.*

Phone doctor

If a pregnant woman, premature baby, person with a compromised immune system or other susceptible condition is exposed to chicken pox, he or she may be advised to take *Varicella zoster* immune globulin (VZIG).

Prevention: Young children should have a single dose of the vaccine when they are receiving their other immunizations, before entering school. Any adult who has not had chicken pox should get two doses of chicken pox vaccine, four to eight weeks apart. The vaccine for chicken pox is 70% to 90% effective, and the few vaccinated individuals who later develop chicken pox have a milder illness. Most children and adults can take the chicken pox vaccine safely. *Pregnant women and anyone with cancer or an illness that harms the immune system should not be vaccinated.*

Get vaccinated

Chicken pox can be spread by coughing or sneezing and contact with the blisters, so an infected person should be kept from contact with persons who have not been vaccinated.

Childbirth, complications of

Normal childbirth
As a fetus approaches birth, it should move into position with its head down. Just before birth, the fetus turns and faces the mother's back, but if there is premature rupture of the membranes, the birth process begins before the fetus has reached the correct position.

Childbirth used to be a very dangerous process, resulting in the deaths of many mothers and babies. Thanks to modern medicine it is now remarkably safe. The rate of death for newborn babies is quite low, and for mothers, even lower. Nevertheless, certain conditions known as complications may occur before, during, or immediately after birth. These may require special medical attention to prevent death or lasting harm. Among the more serious complications are the following.

Preterm birth: One of the greatest dangers a baby can encounter is birth before full term—that is, before the body systems are mature enough to ensure survival. The lungs of a baby born too early may not be able to breathe air, the body itself may not generate enough heat for warmth, and the digestive system may not be able to transform food into nourishment.

Bed rest, certain drugs, and other measures may help prevent or slow premature labor. If premature delivery is considered imminent, corticosteroid drugs given to the mother may help speed up development of the baby's lungs. When preterm birth does occur, facilities dedicated to intensive care for infants can help keep babies alive until their systems develop.

Premature rupture of membranes (PROM): Normally, when pregnancy reaches full term, the "bag of waters," the balloonlike sac of membranes around the baby in the uterus, breaks and releases amniotic fluid either just before or just after labor begins. Sometimes, however, the membranes break open prematurely.

There are two types of premature rupture of membranes. In the more common type the baby is mature, but the break and resulting flow of amniotic fluid occur an hour or more before labor begins. Without the protection of the membrane sac the baby runs an increased risk of infection. Without the cushion of amniotic fluid the umbilical cord is more likely to be compressed (see below). The standard treatment is to hasten delivery by chemically induced labor or by surgical delivery (*cesarean section*).

The second type is called preterm premature rupture of membranes. It occurs before the fetus is fully developed and is likely to trigger preterm birth. A balanced medical strategy must be employed. On the one hand, medications and other methods

On the Internet

MUSC
(Medical University of South
Carolina) CHILDREN'S HOSPITAL

www.musckids.com/
health_library/pregnant/
complcat.htm

are used to delay delivery until development is more complete; on the other, if infection or other threats become serious, immediate delivery may be necessary even if the baby is premature.

Abnormal presentation: Most babies, by the time they are ready to be born, are positioned head down in the uterus facing the mother's back. This is the safest and easiest presentation for birth. Other positions, with the head up and the legs or buttocks down (called *breech presentation*), cause difficulties with delivery and may require cesarean section.

Cephalopelvic (sehf-uh-loh-PEHL-vihk) **disproportion:** The largest single part of a baby is its head. Sometimes the head (*cephalos* in Greek) is too big to pass through the ring of the mother's *pelvic bones*. If the disproportion is severe enough, a cesarean delivery may be necessary.

Umbilical cord compression: Until a baby is born and breathing air, the hollow umbilical cord between the placenta and the baby's navel is a vital lifeline for the delivery of oxygen. Without a steady supply of oxygen the baby will suffer dangerous *hypoxia* (see below).

Before or during labor the cord may become compressed— squeezed so that blood circulation through it is reduced or cut off. The cord may be tightly wrapped around the baby's body, or it may slip forward (*prolapse*) into the birth canal and get trapped between the baby and the canal wall. The cord can sometimes be freed during ordinary delivery, but an emergency cesarean may be necessary.

Asphyxia and hypoxia: Before birth all the oxygen that a baby needs must be supplied by the mother, carried in blood and transferred through the placenta and umbilical cord. At birth this source is cut off, and oxygen must be absorbed from the baby's own lungs.

If the oxygen supply is interrupted, the baby quickly suffers oxygen deprivation, or asphyxia. The resulting lack of oxygen in the body tissues, known as hypoxia, may cause death or permanent damage. For example, hypoxia is thought to trigger bleeding into the brain, which in turn is believed to be a major cause of cerebral palsy, epilepsy, and hydrocephalus.

Before birth asphyxia may result from several conditions, ranging from preeclampsia to prolonged labor. The main solution is to deliver the baby as soon as possible, by cesarean section if necessary.

If a newborn baby does not breathe properly, *resuscitation* measures are used to prevent asphyxia (see Respiratory distress below).

Respiratory distress: For any of several reasons a newborn baby may have trouble breathing properly, a condition known as respiratory distress. The baby might have *wet lung syndrome,* for example: The lungs fail to become entirely free of the fluid that filled them before birth and cannot absorb enough oxygen. Or the airways may be clogged or irritated by *meconium* (mih-KOH-nee-um), waste material released from the baby's bowel into the amniotic fluid. Or the normal flow of nervous impulses that control breathing may be impaired, causing temporary *apnea* (AAP-nee-uh), or "non-breathing."

A variety of resuscitation measures are used to stimulate breathing and to ensure a supply of oxygen to the lungs. They range from simply massaging the chest and suctioning out meconium to providing oxygen mechanically.

Persistent pulmonary hypertension: Before a baby's birth the lungs are inactive, and only a small amount of blood is required to fulfill their needs. The *pulmonary blood vessels* serving the lungs are constricted, raising the pressure but lowering the volume of blood passing through them. This pattern of high blood pressure and low blood flow in the lungs combined with low blood pressure and high blood flow through the rest of the body is known as *fetal circulation.*

At birth a major shift in circulation normally occurs. The lungs expand and fill with air. The pulmonary blood vessels relax and *dilate* (open), lowering blood pressure in the lungs and increasing blood flow, circulating enough blood to absorb oxygen from the lungs. But occasionally, for a variety of reasons, the shift fails to take place when it should. The pulmonary vessels remain constricted (narrow), so lung blood pressure remains high and blood flow low. Without sufficient blood to absorb oxygen from the lungs the baby may suffer asphyxia and hypoxia (see above). This condition is known as persistent pulmonary hypertension, or *persistent fetal circulation.*

Treatment has two aims. The first is to increase flow through the pulmonary blood vessels. Drugs and other techniques are used to dilate blood vessels and stimulate the heart. The other aim is to increase the oxygen supply to the lungs using the resuscitation techniques applied to asphyxia generally.

Group B streptococcus infection: The human body is normally colonized by many kinds of bacteria, most of which are harmless. Among them are Group B streptococcus bacteria, which periodically colonize the lower intestine in men and women or the vagina in women. Group B streptococci tend to cause disease only among those with weak immune systems. Unfortunately, this group includes newborns, whose immune systems are not completely developed. Up to a third of women may be carriers of Group B strep when they go into labor, and a significant percentage of their babies may become infected during delivery.

Group B streptococcus infection is potentially very dangerous to newborns. It can cause sepsis ("blood poisoning"), pneumonia, or meningitis, which may be fatal or result in lasting disabilities.

The infection can be effectively treated with antibiotics, but prevention is better for overall health and safety. Pregnant women can be tested for the bacteria during late pregnancy and early labor and then given antibiotics to reduce or eliminate the bacteria population. Such screening and treatment are becoming increasingly routine.

Postpartum bleeding: After delivery natural contractions of the mother's uterus usually squeeze shut the blood vessels that formerly supplied it, so that normal postpartum bleeding, called *lochia* (LOH-kee-uh), occurs but is gradually reduced. Massage and administration of a hormone that encourages contractions are often used to help the process along. But sometimes dangerously heavy bleeding does occur. Excessive bleeding is treated with drugs that encourage clotting and, in rare instances, with surgery to close the blood vessels.

Chlamydia

(klaa-MIHD-ee-uh)

It is the most common reported disease in the United States, yet more than three-quarters of the women and almost half of the men who have it have no symptoms. The disease is chlamydia.

Cause: Chlamydia is caused by a bacterium, *Chlamydia trachomatis*. Most cases of chlamydia infection are the result of sexual transmission. If a woman has chlamydia during pregnancy, it can be passed to her offspring and cause blindness or severe pneumonia.

Incidence and risk factors: Physicians estimate that some 2.8 million new infections occurred in the United States in 2004, making it the most common sexually transmitted disease.

Chlamydia is most frequently seen in 15 to 24 year olds. Risk factors include having more than one sex partner or a sex partner who has had many partners, having sex without a condom, and having a history of sexually transmitted diseases. Sexually abused children are also at high risk for chlamydia infection.

Noticeable symptoms: Symptoms of chlamydia are different in men and women. About 85% of women have no symptoms. Those who do may experience an abnormal discharge from the vagina, abdominal pain, bleeding between menstrual periods, and painful urination. Only 40% of men have no symptoms. Symptoms in most men consist of a discharge from the penis, painful or burning urination, and tender or swollen testicles.

Diagnosis: The symptoms of chlamydia are similar to those of gonorrhea. The doctor will do tests to determine exactly which sexually transmitted disease the person has, since treatments for chlamydia and gonorrhea are different. Swabs from the opening to the penis or from the vagina and cervix can be taken to get fluid for testing. A urine test may also be used.

Course of the disease: When symptoms occur, they may begin one to two weeks after infection. Prompt treatment is important because serious medical problems can occur if chlamydia infection is not treated. In women the infection can move into the upper part of the reproductive system and spread to the fallopian tubes and ovaries. It can also lead to pelvic inflammatory disease (PID), which can cause blockages in the fallopian tubes. Blocked tubes can result in pregnancy outside the uterus (ectopic pregnancy) or infertility.

In men untreated chlamydia infection can spread to the sperm ducts and cause sterility. About 1% of men with untreated chlamydia infection develop *Reiter's syndrome*—an infection of the urethra—sores on the penis and in the mouth, *conjunctivitis,* and *arthritis.*

Treatment: Chlamydia can be easily and effectively treated with antibiotics. Some effective antibiotics require only one dose; others must be taken daily for a week. It is important that both partners be treated at the same time and that they take the full course of medication. People being treated for chlamydia should abstain from sex during treatment and be checked by a doctor before beginning to have sex again.

Prevention: Like all sexually transmitted diseases, the only sure prevention is abstinence. For people who are sexually active, using either male or female condoms regularly is the best protection. Vaginal spermicidal gels and creams can also help, but they are not as effective as condoms. There is also some evidence that spermicidal creams and gels that contain nonoxynol-9 can cause irritation that increases the risk of HIV infection. For this reason some doctors recommend the use only of creams and gels that do not contain nonoxynol-9. Condoms with nonoxynol-9 are still considered safe because the concentrations are much lower than in creams and gels.

People who are at high risk for chlamydia infection are encouraged to get regular screening (once or twice a year) for chlamydia as well as for other sexually transmitted diseases.

Global impact: Sexually transmitted diseases are a major problem throughout the world. The World Health Organization estimates that there are 92 million cases of chlamydia infection each year. Both industrialized and developing countries are affected, with people in their teens and twenties most likely to be infected.

Chloracne

(klawr-AAK-nee)

SYMPTOM

See also
Cancers
Environment and disease
Skin diseases

Chloracne, a chemically induced skin condition, is the only completely established effect on human beings of the chemicals known as dioxins. The best-known dioxin is a contaminant of a herbicide, but others occur in various chemicals that humans manufacture. These chemicals include some paints and varnishes and some oils used as lubricants in cutting tools.

Parts affected: Chloracne is a serious skin rash that appears on the face or on parts of the body that are exposed to dioxins or to many other chemical compounds based on chlorine. Ingestion or inhalation of dioxins also causes the symptom. The skin condition appears as blackheads and pimples on the face and neck or other parts of the body that have been exposed, often bare arms and hands. It may not respond to treatments for ordinary acne and may persist for many years after exposure to dioxin.

Related symptoms: Dioxins are considered among the most dangerous chemicals because even tiny amounts kill many different animals; effects on humans, other than inducing chloracne, have been hard to establish. Limited statistical evidence suggests that in humans dioxins may increase cancer rates, especially for soft-tissue cancers, lymphomas, multiple myeloma, or cancer of the liver or gallbladder.

Associations: There are about 75 dioxins that are produced at high temperatures in various chemical processes. Therefore they contaminate incinerator ashes as well as chlorine-based chemicals manufactured using high temperatures, such as bleaches used in making white paper. The most famous dioxin is 2,3,7,8-TCDD, a contaminant of insecticides and herbicides. It is the dioxin that contaminated the Agent Orange herbicide used by American soldiers to defoliate forests during the Vietnam War.

Prevention and possible actions: Chloracne occurs only in people who are exposed to chlorinated chemicals. Avoid contact with pesticides completely, and wash thoroughly soon after any contact with liquid paints, varnishes, or cutting oils.

Cholera

(KOL-ehr-uh)

DISEASE

TYPE: INFECTIOUS
(BACTERIAL)

See also
Bacteria and disease
Diarrhea
Epidemics

On the Internet
CENTERS FOR DISEASE CONTROL
AND PREVENTION (CDC)
www.cdc.gov/ncidod/dbmd/
diseaseinfo/cholera_g.htm

Phone doctor

Cholera is a serious intestinal disorder that causes severe diarrhea and vomiting. It is most common in less-developed countries that have poor sanitation facilities. People often get the disease as a result of drinking water contaminated with cholera bacteria. Foods such as shellfish and raw fruits and vegetables may also harbor the bacteria.

Cause: A comma-shaped bacterium called *Vibrio cholerae* causes cholera. Once vibrio bacteria are swallowed, they infect the mucous membrane of the small intestine. A toxin produced by the bacteria then makes bodily fluids flow quickly from the bloodstream into the intestines. Sudden, severe diarrhea and dehydration follow, leading to serious problems if left untreated.

Incidence: Cholera is rare in the United States. The few cases reported each year usually involve travelers returning from Asia or Africa, where the disease is far more widespread and has been known for centuries. Cholera also occurs in South and Central America, as well as in areas around the Mediterranean. In the 1800s worldwide epidemics periodically killed millions; epidemics today still kill thousands.

Noticeable symptoms: About one to five days after initial infection one may experience nausea, dizziness, and anxiousness. Next a watery, grayish-colored diarrhea begins. As much as a pint of water an hour may be lost as the diarrhea continues. Vomiting, without any feeling of nausea, often accompanies the diarrhea. If allowed to continue, the dehydration resulting from the diarrhea leads to intense thirst, muscle cramps, cold and withered skin, and more serious symptoms. *Seek medical help immediately.*

Diagnosis: Eliminating other causes of severe diarrhea and vomiting is an important part of diagnosing cholera. If you have recently returned from a country where cholera outbreaks are common, your doctor probably will suspect it. But a sample of your watery stool, which your doctor will send to a medical lab for testing, will probably be needed to confirm the presence of vibrio bacteria.

Treatment options: Replacing lost body fluids is an essential part of treating cholera and should begin soon after the diarrhea begins. Patients usually drink prescribed amounts of water containing sugar and certain other nutrients to restore the fluids that the diarrhea has drained out. If dehydration develops despite this treatment, the physician may decide to give fluids intravenously as well. Tetracycline hydrochloride or other antibiotics administered early on can help shorten the length of time one suffers with diarrhea.

Prevention: Although cholera vaccines are available in some countries, they give only limited protection, and their use is not recommended by the U.S. Centers for Disease Control and Prevention. As with many other waterborne infectious diseases, travelers must be careful about drinking contaminated water. As a general rule it is probably best to avoid local drinking water outside the United States and Canada. Only bottled drinks or drinking water that has been boiled can be considered safe in nations with poor sanitation. Watch out for ice in drinks as well. Cholera bacteria can also live for several days on fruits and vegetables, so these should not be eaten raw when the source is a location with endemic cholera.

Cholesterol and triglycerides

REFERENCE

Eat low-fat foods

Exercise

An elevated level of cholesterol or triglycerides in the blood is a serious risk factor for cardiovascular disease. Yet more than half of American adults have higher-than-desirable blood levels of these substances—a problem that often begins in childhood. The good news is that a healthy lifestyle can prevent or reduce this risk.

Cholesterol is a soft, waxy, fatlike substance found in body cells and essential for life. It conducts messages along nerves and is needed for the function and repair of cell membranes and the production of vitamin D and certain hormones. The liver makes cholesterol but cholesterol also enters the body in foods we eat. Foods that contain high levels of saturated fat (such as red meats, cheese, and eggs) or high levels of cholesterol (such as shellfish, liver, and egg yolks) increase blood levels of cholesterol. Fruit, grains, and other foods of plant origin do not contain cholesterol.

See also
Atherosclerosis
Diet and health
Exercise
Hardening of the arteries

On the Internet
WEB MD
www.webmd.com/hw/
cholesterol_management/
hw207814.asp

There are two types of cholesterol. *Low-density lipoprotein* or LDL cholesterol is often called the "bad" kind. It collects on artery walls and leads to the formation of plaque, which blocks arteries and reduces blood flow. Eating foods laden with saturated fats or cholesterol increases LDL levels.

High-density lipoprotein or HDL cholesterol is the "good" kind. It helps remove LDL from artery walls, thereby reversing some of the latter's bad effects. Omega-3 fat, found in fatty cold water fish, soybeans, and walnuts, helps raise HDL levels. So too does vigorous exercise, losing weight, and stopping smoking.

Triglycerides are a type of fat stored in fat cells and released to meet the body's energy needs between meals. The body obtains them from fats in foods and also makes them from carbohydrates. As with LDL, high triglyceride levels are harmful. Aerobic exercise, losing excess weight, and eating less sugar and saturated fats can help lower triglyceride levels.

Associations: People with high LDL cholesterol and triglyceride levels are at risk of high blood pressure and atherosclerosis—both of which significantly increase the risk for heart attack and stroke. High cholesterol also has been associated with increased risk of dementia in later life.

	Blood level (mg/dL)	What it means
Total cholesterol	Less than 200	Desirable
	230–239	Borderline high
	240 or higher	High
LDL	Less than 100*	Optimal
	100–129	Near optimal
	130–159	Borderline high
	160 or higher	High
HDL	Less than 40	Low
	40–59	Acceptable
	60 or higher	Optimal
Triglycerides	Less than 150	Normal
	150–199	Borderline high
	200 or higher	High

*It is recommended that people at very high risk—for example, those who already have heart disease or diabetes—reduce target LDL levels to less than 70 mg/dL.

Extremely low cholesterol levels can also be harmful. They have been linked to depression and anxiety, and may be an indication of poor health.

Diagnosis: To determine cholesterol and triglyceride levels, blood is drawn from a vein after a person has fasted for 8 to 12 hours. An assay called a lipoprotein profile is done, providing blood levels in milligrams per deciliter (mg/dL) of blood.

Treatment options: For many people who have high cholesterol and triglyceride levels, eating a diet low in saturated fat and cholesterol, getting regular exercise, and losing excess weight are sufficient to lower triglycerides and LDL and raise HDL.

For people who have genetic high cholesterol and others who are unable to reduce levels by diet and exercise alone, a doctor may prescribe medicines called statins.

Chromosomal abnormalities

DISORDER

TYPE: GENETIC

See also
Down syndrome
Fragile X syndrome
Genetic diseases

Within each regular cell of the body is a nucleus that directs the development and operations of that cell. The nucleus in human cells contains 46 chromosomes (KRO-muh-sohms). These chromosomes not only have the instruction set for cell operations, they also contain the genetic instructions—the genes—that determine the physical traits you inherit from your parents. Half the chromosomes come from each parent—23 from the father and 23 from the mother. The pairs are combined when the mother's egg is fertilized by the father's sperm.

Sometimes an abnormality occurs in either the formation or the combination of the chromosomes. The fertilized egg ends up with too many or too few chromosomes, or with chromosomes that are mixed or scrambled in some way.

Because each chromosome contains many genes, chromosomal abnormalities are likely to cause serious birth defects, affecting many body systems and often including developmental disability (mental retardation). Many of these defects are so severe that the offspring receiving them cannot survive. Of the abnormalities that do allow survival, the best known is Down

NORMAL CHROMOSOMES

1	2	3	4	5
6	7	8	9 10 11 12	
13	14	15	16 17 18	19 20
	21	22	X	Y

ABNORMAL CHROMOSOMES

–extra portion
14

–extra copy
21

Chromosome pairs

The 23 pairs of chromosomes direct heredity and cell operations. When one chromosome combines with part of another or when there is an extra chromosome, development is seriously affected.

syndrome, which occurs when an extra copy of one specific chromosome is inherited, making a triplet instead of a pair.

There is one major exception to the rule that chromosomal abnormalities are noticeable at birth. Abnormalities in the number of the male (Y) or female (X) chromosomes that determine the off-spring's sex tend to be far less severe. Sex-chromosome abnormalities include Klinefelter syndrome among boys (XXY or sometimes XXXY) and Turner syndrome among girls (one X, no Y).

Cause: No one knows exactly what causes chromosomal abnormalities to occur in particular fertilized eggs. Most occurrences appear to be accidental, caused by improper division of the cells that give rise to eggs or sperm.

Incidence: Scientists are just beginning to find out how common chromosomal abnormalities are. A large percentage of fetuses miscarry in early pregnancy, and it turns out that many of these have chromosomal abnormalities that prevent survival.

Noticeable symptoms: Chromosomal abnormalities (other than those that affect the sex chromosomes) are almost sure to be noticeable at birth.

Diagnosis: Microscopic examination of the chromosomes in a nucleus clearly shows such abnormalities. They can be identified before birth in fetal cells collected during a *prenatal test* such as amniocentesis (AAM-nee-oh-sehn-TEE-sihs).

Treatment options: Chromosomal abnormalities cannot be cured. Some symptoms, such as heart and digestive system malformations that are common in Down syndrome, can be remedied with surgery or other medical treatment.

Outlook: The outlook for affected children varies enormously. Some with sex-chromosome abnormalities lead entirely normal lives. At the other extreme are those so severely affected that they die before or shortly after birth. Even for a particular type of abnormality, such as Down syndrome, there is a wide range of abilities and physical conditions.

Risk factors: Chromosomal abnormalities are weakly familial: They occur more often in certain families, but not often enough to establish a clear pattern of inheritance. The main risk factor is the mother's age. Chromosomal abnormalities become increasingly common from the time the mother is 35 years old.

Chronic fatigue syndrome

DISEASE

TYPE: UNKNOWN CAUSE

See also
Candidiasis
Clinical depression
Fibromyalgia
Immune system
Mononucleosis
Viruses and disease

On the Internet
CENTERS FOR DISEASE CONTROL
AND PREVENTION (CDC)
www.cdc.gov/ncidod/diseases/cfs/

Characterized by unexplained, prolonged fatigue, chronic fatigue syndrome, or CFS, is a mysterious condition that has been known by many names over the years, including chronic mononucleosis and yuppie flu. In England it is called myalgic encephalitis, while in Japan it is known as natural killer cell syndrome.

Cause: Medical researchers have not yet determined the cause of CFS. It is possible that a virus infection, such as Epstein-Barr virus, plays a role but there is no evidence that the disease is contagious. Other causes that have been suggested include iron-deficiency anemia, a history of allergies, hypoglycemia (low blood sugar), and a dysfunction of the immune system. Some studies show that CFS may be linked to a kind of low blood pressure called *neurally mediated hypotension*. The hypotension is not thought to be a cause of CFS, nor CFS of the hypotension, but the symptoms overlap considerably.

Incidence: CFS affects both sexes and all racial and ethnic groups. Although adolescents can have the disease, onset generally occurs between ages 22 and 44. More than twice as many women as men have the condition. Based on several studies, it is estimated that as many as half a million Americans have the disease.

Noticeable symptoms: Not surprisingly, given its official name, the primary symptom of CFS is extreme fatigue or tiredness. This fatigue is so severe that it can interfere with carrying on most usual activities. The feeling of fatigue is also made more intense by exercise, even mild exertion.

Some people with CFS may also develop a recurring sore throat without a discharge and other symptoms that usually go along with the flu. They may have aches and pains in muscles and joints, but in these cases the joints are not swollen or red. Other symptoms are painful lymph nodes in the armpits and neck, headaches, a slight fever, from 99.5°F to 100.5°F, and chills.

People with CFS may also experience the symptoms of depression. They may become confused and irritable and find themselves forgetting things. Typically, short-term memory is affected, but other types of memory impairment, such as absent-mindedness or inability to recall names, is usually not seen.

Despite the extreme fatigue, people with CFS may also have difficulty sleeping; and when sleep does occur, it may not eliminate fatigue.

Diagnosis: Your physician will want to determine the length of time over which you have experienced the symptoms listed above. By the official criteria for CFS from the Centers for Disease Control and Prevention, such fatigue must have had a specific onset and then lasted for at least six months. All other conditions that may cause chronic fatigue must be eliminated, including tuberculosis, cancer, anemia, diabetes, chronic hepatitis B or C infection, heart disease, sleep apnea, eating disorders, and alcohol abuse. In order to eliminate these possibilities, the physician will perform a series of standard medical tests, such as blood tests and x-rays. The physician will also ask if the patient has been diagnosed with any mental disorder marked by fatigue, such as schizophrenia or bipolar disorder.

Finally, the patient must have four or more symptoms from the following list:

■ constant fatigue
■ substantial impairment of short-term memory or noticeable inability to concentrate
■ sore throat
■ tender lymph nodes
■ pain in the muscles
■ pain in more than one joint unaccompanied by redness or swelling
■ headaches that are different from those previously experienced
■ fatigue on awakening after several hours' sleep
■ feeling bad after exercise if that feeling lasts for more than a day

All of these must also have lasted for six months or more and have originated at the same time as the onset of chronic fatigue. Although various medical tests can exclude other causes of the symptoms, no tests are currently available for the specific purpose of diagnosing CFS. Rather, the diagnosis results from eliminating other possibilities. To complicate matters, a number of illnesses have similar symptoms. These include fibromyalgia, chronic mononucleosis, and multiple chemical sensitivities.

Did You Know?

Although people have shown the symptoms of chronic fatigue syndrome for over 200 years, the disease was not officially recognized until 1987.

Treatment options: Just as the cause of CFS has not been determined, no cure has yet been found. In order to make the condition as easy as possible to live with, eat a well-balanced diet, get plenty of rest, and avoid stressful situations and extreme physical exertion. If your symptoms include muscle and joint pains and headaches, you may also take over-the-counter pain relievers. Some people find that avoiding foods with preservatives, dyes, and caffeine alleviates the symptoms.

Physicians have helped people overcome the depression or anxiety that accompanies CFS with antidepressants or with medicines that reduce panic attacks.

Neurally mediated hypotension, if found, may be treated with a diet that is high in salt and water consumption and with medications that raise or steady blood pressure.

Stages and progress: While there is no cure for CFS, it sometimes does go away spontaneously. That is, about half the people with the disease find their symptoms disappear within five years. Others have the symptoms decrease substantially, so that the disease no longer is as likely to interfere with their daily lives. However, for some people the symptoms may recur in full strength periodically over many years.

Circulatory system

BODY SYSTEM

The circulatory system—often called the *vascular* (VAAS-kyuh-luhr) *system* by physicians—is the transport network that carries chemicals and some cells around the body. Its main parts have separate entries in these volumes.

General description: Blood is carried throughout the body in a closed system of tubes known collectively as *blood vessels*. Vessels carrying blood away from the heart are called arteries. The smallest arteries are called *arterioles* (ahr-TIHR-ee-OHLS). Arterioles merge into very tiny tubes called capillaries, whose walls are so thin that oxygen and nutrients pass through to reach cells. Meanwhile carbon dioxide and wastes from the cells pass through into the blood. The waste-carrying blood then enters veins, vessels that lead back to the heart.

An important side loop for the circulatory system pumps blood from the heart to the lungs to pick up fresh oxygen and

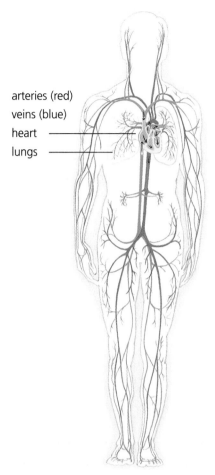

arteries (red)
veins (blue)
heart
lungs

Blood flows from heart to lungs, where it exchanges carbon dioxide for oxygen. The heart then pumps it through the body.

to release accumulated carbon dioxide. After blood has made the trip to the lungs and back, it is directed into the first loop that passes through the rest of the body. Therefore the lungs, heart, and blood vessels may be thought of as a single body system of which the circulatory system is just a part.

Role: Although the primary function of the circulatory system is the transport of oxygen and carbon dioxide, much else is carried along with the blood—energy supplies for cells, water, hormones, minerals, immune system cells and substances, and other necessary materials. The materials include fats and cholesterol needed for building and maintaining cell membranes. And, of course, the blood carries undesirable toxins and infectious agents such as viruses and bacteria, helping to spread disease throughout the body.

Conditions that affect the circulatory system: Any condition or event that halts blood flow soon results in death to the cells that are no longer receiving blood. Dead tissue may deteriorate rapidly, a condition called gangrene. If a vital organ is affected, the interference with blood flow can be fatal.

The most common way that blood flow is blocked is through buildup of material within an artery, as in atherosclerosis or embolism.

Any break in the circulatory system diverts blood from where it is intended to go. Breaks that let blood flow out of the body may be caused by a wound, which if deep also permits blood to leak inside the body. Another cause of diversion of blood is the bursting of a weak spot on an artery. Weak spots usually balloon into an aneurysm before they burst.

Conditions that affect blood pressure, such as hypertension (high blood pressure), can lead to breaks and blockages in the circulatory system. Both types of diabetes mellitus and also tobacco smoking tend to reduce circulation, especially in the hands and feet (the *extremities*), more so when diabetes is combined with smoking. This kind of reduction is termed *peripheral artery disease;* it can interfere with walking or even reduce blood supply so much that cells die and gangrene develops.

Often when circulation is impaired, blood is kept by the vital organs in the trunk and skull, leading to loss of blood supply to the extremities. This can occur for reasons ranging from loss of blood from the system to diseases that reduce blood flow.

Maintaining a healthy circulatory system: Regular physical activity, including aerobic exercise, stimulates the growth of capillaries, ensures that the circulatory system carries a plentiful supply of oxygen to the cells, and significantly decreases the risk of stroke and other cardiovascular diseases. Exercise also helps maintain a healthy weight, which limits stress placed on the heart and blood vessels.

A well-balanced diet rich in fruits, vegetables, and whole grains and low in fats and cholesterol helps prevent the buildup of plaque in artery walls. Certain nutrients are particularly important for the circulatory system. For instance, iron is needed to form the hemoglobin that carries oxygen through the body.

Do not smoke or chew tobacco. Red wine, in moderation, can benefit the circulatory system but otherwise consumption of alcoholic beverages should be limited.

Treat wounds promptly, cleaning them and applying an antiseptic to prevent infection.

Cirrhosis of the liver

(sih-ROH-sihs)

DISEASE

TYPE: CHEMICAL;
     MECHANICAL

Cirrhosis is a liver disease characterized by progressive and usually irreversible scarring of liver tissue. This destroys the liver's ability to carry out many important functions and can lead to death. With treatment and behavioral changes, however, the disease's progress can often be halted.

Cause: Alcohol consumption is the leading cause of cirrhosis in North America and many other developed lands. As alcohol use increases, so does the incidence of cirrhosis. For instance, a sharp jump in alcohol consumption in Britain since the 1970s has been accompanied by increases in cirrhosis death rates, even while the rest of Europe has seen a 20 to 30% decline in such death rates.

The second major cause is chronic infection with hepatitis B or C viruses. In addition to causing scarring, the infections greatly increase the risk of developing a form of liver cancer called *hepatocellular carcinoma*, which arises from hepatocytes, the main cell type in the liver. Although relatively rare in North America, worldwide it is a leading cause of cancer death.

Phone doctor

Incidence: Cirrhosis is a leading cause of death. In the United States liver disease, including cirrhosis, causes about 27,000 deaths annually. Between 10% and 25% of alcoholics develop cirrhosis.

Noticeable symptoms: Very early signs of cirrhosis can be hard to detect, since the disease may begin with general weakness and weight loss. Later symptoms, such as loss of appetite, indigestion, nausea, vomiting, abdominal swelling, intense itching, and a general feeling of ill health, become more noticeable. Cirrhosis patients may get *spider nevi*—spidery red marks—on the upper body, arms, and face. The lack of bile in the digestive system leads to light-colored stools. People with cirrhosis may also begin to bruise and bleed more easily as the disease progresses, since the liver manufactures vital clotting components.

Blockage of the portal vein that carries blood from the rest of the digestive system through the liver causes *hypertension* in the veins of the digestive system; the hypertension can cause distended veins called *varices* (VEHR-uh-SEEZ) in the esophagus and stomach. Such veins often break open, causing profuse bleeding that is a recognizable symptom of cirrhosis.

Cirrhosis is a life-threatening disease. If you or someone in your family experiences the symptoms above, get prompt medical attention.

Diagnosis: A doctor may be able to diagnose cirrhosis based on a patient's past history and a physical examination. But it will be important to determine the primary cause and extent of the liver damage. Blood tests, a liver biopsy (tissue sample), endoscopy to look for varices, ultrasound, and computerized tomography (CT) scans are all employed. The small piece of liver removed during a biopsy will show the extent of the tissue damage. Ultrasound and CT scans provide information on changes in liver size, tumors, and other factors relating to cirrhosis.

Treatment options: Although liver tissue can regenerate, the widespread damage caused by advanced cirrhosis cannot be reversed. Medical treatment can help prevent further damage and maintain liver function at its current level.

Removing the primary cause of the liver damage is the doctor's first priority. Whether cirrhosis was alcohol-induced

12-Step meeting

On the Internet
NATIONAL DIGESTIVE DISEASES
INFORMATION CLEARINGHOUSE
digestive.niddk.nih.gov/
ddiseases/pubs/cirrhosis

or not, drinking must be given up completely. Alcoholics may need the help of a support group such as Alcoholic Anonymous. Adhering to a well-balanced, nutritious diet high in carbohydrates and vitamins and low in fat is also important.

Among the medications the doctor may prescribe are antacids to deal with abdominal discomfort, diuretics to reduce fluid buildup, and, in certain types of cirrhosis, corticosteroids or other immune-system-suppressing drugs. Where there are problems with bleeding, blood transfusions will replace lost blood volume.

People with advanced cirrhosis may be candidates for a liver transplant, in which the patient receives a healthy organ from a recently deceased individual. However, there are not enough donor livers to meet needs. About 80% of liver transplant patients survive at least one year following the operation.

Stages and progress: A healthy liver performs several important bodily functions. It helps control the volume of blood in the body; produces substances needed to make blood clot; regulates fluid amount and chemical balances in blood; neutralizes toxins absorbed by the intestines; and helps convert nutrients in food into a source of energy. But heavy drinking, toxic chemicals, hepatitis, and other agents slowly damage liver tissue. Cirrhosis occurs when enough healthy tissue has been damaged and replaced by scar tissue and fat. The liver simply does not have enough tissue left to perform its vital tasks.

Once the disease reaches its later stages, the patient may begin suffering jaundice, a symptom of liver disease and some other conditions. The skin and whites of the eyes turn a yellowish color. Men lose interest in sex and become impotent, and may develop painfully swollen breasts. Women may stop having their menstrual periods. Fluid builds up in the abdomen and ankles, and the likelihood of bleeding in the esophagus and stomach increases. Liver cancer may develop. Severe bleeding in advanced cases may finally cause death. Complete liver failure is also fatal.

Meanwhile, the decline in liver function also affects the patient's mental state. Irritability, an inability to concentrate, and trembling of the hands all become more noticeable. Later the patient's memory will be impaired. Confusion, delirium, and drowsiness in later stages indicate liver failure.

Avoid alcohol

Prevention: Personal responsibility, including seeking medical help for early alcoholism or hepatitis, can prevent almost all cases of cirrhosis. Excessive regular alcohol consumption or binge drinking should be avoided. Safe sexual practices and not sharing needles for drugs can help prevent hepatitis infections. Vaccinations for hepatitis B and C are recommended. It is important to avoid alcohol during treatment for hepatitis because alcohol damages the immune defense against the virus.

Claudication

See **Leg cramps; Peripheral artery disease**

Cleft lip and palate

DISORDER

TYPE: DEVELOPMENTAL

See also
**Childbirth, complications of
Genetic diseases**

On the Internet
CLEFT PALATE FOUNDATION
www.cleftline.org/aboutclp

The facial features take shape in the early weeks of prenatal development. Parts of the face are formed separately and then join, or fuse, together. Sometimes this process fails to be fully completed, especially in the area of the mouth. The result is a *cleft* (gap) in the upper lip, in the hard palate (the bony roof of the mouth), the soft palate (the area behind the roof of the mouth), or in some combination of these. A cleft lip is sometimes known as *harelip*.

Cause: The causes of cleft lip and cleft palate are unknown. The conditions are familial (they tend to run in families), and they occur more often in certain ethnic groups. But they have no clear pattern of inheritance, so are not considered entirely genetic in origin. Cleft lip and cleft palate may also accompany a wide range of other birth-defect syndromes, some of which are clearly genetic.

Incidence: The most common form of this group of birth defects is a combination of cleft lip and cleft palate. It occurs in 1 out of every 700 to 1,000 infants. It is more common in boys than in girls, and less common among babies of African ancestry than among those of other racial groups.

Noticeable symptoms: Both conditions are clearly evident at birth. Feeding may be difficult for an infant with cleft lip or palate.

Diagnosis: A pediatrician will examine the baby carefully to ascertain the extent of the cleft or clefts and to determine whether they are signs of other birth-defect syndromes.

Treatment: Cleft lip and cleft palate can be remedied by surgery, which is quite effective in repairing these conditions. Initial surgery for cleft lip is usually performed in early infancy and for cleft palate between nine and eighteen months. Additional surgery may be needed in later years. For example, surgery may be done to bring the upper and lower jaws into better alignment.

Related problems may require a team of specialists. For instance, dentists and orthodontists can correct misaligned teeth and replace any missing tooth with an artificial tooth. A speech therapist can provide help in improving speaking skills.

Prevention: Evidence suggests that pregnant women can reduce the risk of cleft lip and palate in their babies by not smoking or drinking and by making sure they get enough vitamins, particularly folic acid. Although there is a genetic component to cleft lip and palate, the presence of the disorder in one child does not appreciably increase the risk for the same disorder in later children of the same parents.

Clinical depression

DISEASE

TYPE: MENTAL; CHEMICAL

See also
Alcoholism
Bipolar disorder
Drug abuse
Mental illnesses
Paranoia
SAD (seasonal affective disorder)
Suicide

Everyone feels discouraged from time to time. Many people report "having the blues" or the "blahs." Few of us get through life without experiencing depression of this sort at one time or another. Clinical depression—also known as *major depression* or *serious depression*—however, is more than just occasionally feeling sad. Sufferers feel sad all the time. They are pessimistic, have a sense of hopelessness, and lack interest in once-pleasurable activities. They may lose their desire to live and their thoughts may turn to suicide. The good news is that although clinical depression is among the most common of all mental diseases, it also is one of the most treatable.

Major depression can occur alone or can alternate with episodes of excitement known as manic behavior. The alternating manic-depressive illness is called bipolar disorder; it responds to different medications from those used for clinical depression. Another, somewhat milder, depressive disease occurs only during winter months when daylight hours are short; it is called SAD (seasonal affective disorder).

Cause: Clinical depression involves chemicals in the brain called *neurotransmitters,* which carry messages between nerve cells.

Scientists have found connections between clinical depression and three neurotransmitters: serotonin, norepinephrine, and dopamine. These neurotransmitters regulate emotions, sleep, appetite, and reactions to stress. If their levels in the brain are too high or too low, a person may become depressed.

There is no single cause for clinical depression, and in some cases the cause that triggers the illness cannot be determined. Factors that have been identified as playing a role include genetics, medical conditions, life events, environmental conditions, and certain thinking patterns.

Depression runs in families, which suggests that some people who become depressed have inherited genes that increase the risk of the disease. For instance, a person might inherit a risk of producing insufficient amounts of norepinephrine.

Illness can be accompanied by clinical depression that goes beyond distress over the disease itself. Stroke, cancer, diabetes, epilepsy, mononucleosis, and hepatitis are closely linked to depression. Hormonal changes, such as those that youngsters experience during puberty, and hormone imbalances, such as those of hypothyroidism (an underactive thyroid gland), can be factors. Hormonal changes before, during, and following childbirth can contribute to postpartum depression, which usually lasts a few days to a few weeks.

Often, depression is a side effect of drugs such as tranquilizers, sleeping pills, blood pressure medications, and steroids; removing the medication or adjusting its dosage can usually cure the problem. Other drugs that are depressants and often abused include alcohol and heroin.

Traumatic events, including child abuse, divorce, or the death of a beloved family member or friend, sometimes lead to depression. So, too, can difficult environmental conditions, including stressful family or work situations, community violence, poverty, and war.

Incidence: Studies suggest that between 8% and 17% of the world's adult population suffer from clinical depression. Part of the difficulty in obtaining more exact data is the fact that a majority of people with the disease go undiagnosed.

Clinical depression can affect people of all ages, races, and socioeconomic standing. Females experience the condition twice as often as males; some studies indicate that 20% or more of women are affected at some point in their lives. Among adolescents, girls are more likely than boys to develop symptoms. The incidence of postpartum depression is similar to depression in women generally, although the incidence in the first month following childbirth is three times the average monthly incidence in nonchildbearing women.

Noticeable symptoms: Three kinds of symptoms can occur: emotional, behavioral, and physical.

Emotional symptoms may include great sadness, hopelessness, pessimism, and guilt. The depressed person may lose interest in the people and activities around him and may not be able to see the good side of anything. Crying spells may ensue.

Phone doctor

Behavioral symptoms may include irritability, poor memory, and inability to concentrate. Some people experience symptoms of psychosis, such as hallucinations or paranoia.

Physical symptoms may include loss of appetite, weight changes, headaches, and trouble sleeping.

If such symptoms persist for two weeks or longer, suicide may become problematic. ***If you feel suicidal, seek medical assistance immediately.***

The progress of clinical depression differs greatly. Some people have only one episode during a lifetime, while others have repeated incidents. In some people an episode lasts a few weeks; in others it lasts for months or years.

Diagnosis: Mental illnesses are diagnosed according to specific criteria. Your physician will look for five or more of the following symptoms that have persisted for two weeks or more:

- persistent low, anxious, or empty feelings
- decreased energy, fatigue, a feeling of being slowed down
- loss of interest or pleasure in usual activities, including sex
- insomnia, early morning waking, oversleeping, or other sleep disturbances
- significant appetite change or weight change (either loss or gain)
- feelings of hopelessness or pessimism
- feelings of guilt, worthlessness, or helplessness
- thoughts of death or suicide
- difficulty in concentrating, remembering, or making decisions
- chronic aches or pains without physical origin

Since there are many diseases that can cause depression, your doctor will want to check you carefully to rule them out. Since some prescription drugs can trigger depression, tell your physician about every medication you take.

Treatment options: The great majority of people who suffer depression can be helped by appropriate treatment, although many of them will have another episode at a later time.

Most clinical depression is controlled with antidepressant medicines, psychotherapy, or a combination of the two.

Antidepressants work on one or more neurotransmitters. For example, selective serotonin reuptake inhibitors (SSRIs)—including Prozac, Paxil, and Zoloft—change the way the brain handles serotonin. Many newer antidepressants, such as serotonin-norepinephrine reuptake inhibitors (SNRIs), work on multiple neurotransmitters. Older antidepressants still prescribed are the tricyclic antidepressants. Because people react differently to medications, doctors carefully monitor patients to make sure they are receiving the appropriate drugs and dosage.

Talking with a psychotherapist or other mental health professional helps patients understand depression and what they can do to control it. It can help reorient a person whose life and relationships have been altered by depression.

Some dietary supplements appear to be helpful in combating depression. These include omega-3 fatty acids, folic acid, and vitamin B_{12}. Light therapy and hypnotherapy may also help, at least temporarily. If other treatments fail, electroconvulsive therapy (ECT), in which an electrical current is passed through the brain, is often effective.

Prevention: If you begin to feel depressed, here are some steps that may help. Avoid alcohol and illicit drugs, exercise regularly, and expose yourself to bright light, either indoors or out. Carry out activities that you normally enjoy and stay involved with other people. Avoid making major decisions while you are depressed. Stop taking drugs other than those prescribed by a physician. These steps coupled with a few days' time usually help ordinary depression. *If symptoms of depression last two weeks or longer, see your doctor or a psychological counselor.*

Avoid alcohol

Phone doctor

Exercise

Cloning and disease

REFERENCE

See also
Diabetes mellitus, type 1
Genetic engineering
Genome
Immune system
Organ transplants
Parkinson's disease
Reproduction
Stem cells

On the Internet
HUMAN GENOME PROGRAM
www.ornl.gov/sci/techresources/
Human_Genome/elsi/
cloning.shtml

A *clone* is an organism that has exactly the same genetic make-up as another from which it is derived. A plant grown from a stem or leaf, for example, is a clone. Most animals cannot be cloned from a part, but scientists have developed methods for cloning fish, amphibians, reptiles, and some mammals using eggs. The first cloned mammal was a sheep in 1997.

Reproductive cloning: In reproductive cloning, the nucleus—which contains the genome—is removed from an egg from one individual. The nucleus of a cell from a different individual is inserted in its place. The altered egg is implanted into a female so that it can grow and be born in the normal way. The new baby is a clone of the individual whose nucleus was inserted into the egg. Usually many attempts must be made to produce a single clone; often hundreds of eggs are used and fail to develop properly before there is a success.

Most scientists believe that it would be unethical to clone a human, but some believe that the first part of the process might be used to create stem cells. The first few generations of cells, called embryonic stem cells, can grow into any tissues of the body. When embryonic stem cells are implanted into an organ, the biochemical environment causes them to grow into tissues found in that organ. Such a procedure might cure diabetes mellitus, type 1, by replacing lost insulin-producing cells, or Parkinson's disease, by introducing cells that produce dopamine.

Therapeutic cloning: The immune system is likely to attack tissue from implanted stem cells as foreign. However, if a cell nucleus from a person needing new tissue is used to clone the stem cells, the genomes match and there is no immune attack. This process is called therapeutic cloning. Scientists could direct cells from the clone to form specific tissues, which then could be implanted. A patient might have cloned cardiac tissue used instead of a heart transplant or cloned liver cells instead of a liver transplant. Since the immune system recognizes the therapeutic clone as "self," the patient would not need to use immune-suppressing drugs for a lifetime, which is necessary when organs have been transplanted from a different individual. There are many steps yet to be taken before therapeutic cloning becomes practical, however.

Clubfoot and related problems

DISORDER

TYPE: DEVELOPMENTAL

See also
**Childbirth, complications of
Foot problems**

On the Internet
MASSACHUSETTS GENERAL
HOSPITAL
www.massgeneral.org/ortho/
ClubFoot.htm

Among the most common birth defects are deformities of the feet. They may occur in one or both feet and can eventually cause walking difficulties that range from almost unnoticeable to severely crippling. Three of these conditions are especially prevalent.

- *Clubfoot,* technically known as *equinovarus* (EH-kwiy-noh-VAY-ruhs), is the most serious. The foot is twisted inward and downward, and the condition will not improve with time. If it is not successfully treated, the afflicted child will not be able to place the sole flat on the ground but will have to walk on the ball or the side of the foot. Normal growth is also hindered. If just one foot is affected, that foot will be smaller than the other, and the leg will be shorter.
- *Calcaneus valgus* (kaal-KAY-nee-uhs VAAL-guhs) is the most common of these defects. The affected foot is angled upward and outward. The condition is relatively mild and usually goes away by itself. Otherwise it may eventually cause the child to walk on the heel or the inner side of the foot.
- *Metatarsus varus* or *adductus* (MEHT-uh-TAAR-suhs VAAR-uhs or ah-DUK-tuhs) is also relatively mild and generally resolves itself over time. The front of the affected foot turns inward; this may eventually cause awkwardness in walking or running.

Cause: Calcaneus valgus and metatarsus adductus are considered to be *deformations* that occur during later prenatal development. That is, one or both feet get cramped and twisted in a constricted uterus. Clubfoot, on the other hand, is thought to be a *malformation* of early development in which the tendons and ligaments of the foot and ankle fail to form properly. Clubfoot tends to appear more often in certain families but is not clearly genetic.

Incidence: All these defects are fairly common. Clubfoot occurs in about 1 in 1,000 babies, metatarsus adductus in about 1 in 1,000 to 2,000, and calcaneus valgus even more often.

Noticeable symptoms: These defects are usually visible at birth.

Diagnosis: X-rays and other special tests may be used to determine the nature and severity of the defects.

Treatment: Mild defects may merit no other care than careful monitoring until they disappear by themselves. More severe defects may require remedial treatment, starting soon after birth, so that the baby will not have difficulties when beginning to walk.

Stretching. Calcaneus valgus and metatarsus adductus can sometimes be corrected by simple stretching exercises performed on the child's feet by a parent.

Casts. The most common treatment for foot deformities is to manipulate the foot into the most normal position possible without causing pain and then to apply a plaster cast to hold the foot immobile in that position. The process is repeated every two weeks or so until the position is normal. Then a splint is used to preserve the change.

Surgery. Severe clubfoot may require surgery to repair the defective tendons and ligaments.

Outlook: Once even a severe foot deformity is treated, the child can usually walk normally.

Cluster headaches

DISEASE

TYPE: COMBINATION

See also
Headache
Migraine
Pain

On the Internet
AMERICAN ACADEMY
OF FAMILY PHYSICIANS
familydoctor.org/035.xml

Cluster headaches take their name from their characteristic pattern of occurrence. Attacks are concentrated in periodic clusters, usually from one to three times a day for one to two months. These clusters are followed by periods of remission that last anywhere from several months to several years. Some persons, however, experience daily headaches for as long as a year.

Attacks come on suddenly and without warning. They last from half an hour to two hours and then quickly subside. They tend to be repeated at the same times each day and often occur at night. The headaches affect only one side of the head, usually in the area nearest the eye. Sufferers describe the pain as excruciatingly intense.

Attacks may be accompanied by other symptoms. In particular, the eye on the affected side may become red and gush tears, the eyelid may droop, and the nose may become clogged with mucus.

Most cluster headaches are *episodic;* the clusters alternate with periods of remission. In a minority of cases the condition becomes *chronic,* with little or no relief between daily attacks. Each of these two forms can switch to the other.

Cause: The cause of cluster headaches is unknown. They were once thought to be closely related to migraine but now appear to be a separate disorder. There are several clues that suggest the cause may be related to biological rhythms, since the attacks tend to occur at the same time of the day. The immune system may be involved as small changes in histamine levels and immune system skin cells have been detected. Some changes in levels of neurotransmitters have also been observed.

Incidence: Cluster headaches are uncommon but not rare. By one estimate about 1 in 1,450 people suffer from them. Men are five to six times more likely than women to be affected.

Noticeable symptoms: The clustered attacks of intense pain, occurring on just one side of the head at about the same times each day, are unmistakable.

Diagnosis: There are no special tests for cluster headaches. They are generally diagnosed from symptoms reported by the sufferer, supplemented by observation of related effects such as a red, teary eye with a drooping eyelid.

Treatment: Symptomatic treatment aims to relieve pain during an attack and to cut the attack short. Since attacks come with little or no warning, ordinary painkillers, even opioids such as codeine, are ineffective, in large part because they take effect too slowly. The most widely used drugs are those that regulate the function of serotonin, such as sumatriptan, which can be self-injected, and ergotamine, which can be inhaled. Inhaling pure oxygen is also effective.

Prevention: Regular and restful sleep helps reduce attacks. Also, since most people who suffer these headaches drink alcohol and smoke tobacco, it is thought that stopping both habits—a good idea for other reasons as well—can help. Sometimes a particular food appears to trigger an attack.

The corticosteroid prednisone, sometimes combined with ergotamine, is the most common drug used to prevent attacks. Other drugs include methysergide, a chemical relative of ergotamine, and verapamil, a calcium channel blocker used in the treatment of hypertension and heart disease. For chronic cluster headaches compounds of lithium, also used to treat bipolar disorder, appear to be especially effective. Both prednisone and lithium can have undesirable side effects and must be monitored carefully by a physician.

Outlook: Once they begin, cycles of cluster headaches tend to persist throughout life. In many cases, however, treatment can substantially reduce the intensity and frequency of attacks.

Cold sore

DISEASE

TYPE: INFECTIOUS (VIRAL)

See also
Canker
Chicken pox
Genital herpes
Shingles
Viruses and disease

On the Internet
KIDS HEALTH
kidshealth.org/kid/
health_problems/teeth/
cold_sores.html

Small sores that develop on the lips or within the mouth may be cold sores, also called *fever blisters*. Cold sores are highly contagious and should not be confused with cankers, which are not contagious. Sores of any type, as well as wounds, are also called *lesions* (LEE-zhuhnz).

Cause: A virus known as *Herpes simplex* causes cold sores. Usually, cold sores result from the herpes type I strain, which is slightly different from the type II strain that causes genital herpes. The herpes family of viruses also causes chicken pox and shingles.

One can become infected with herpes type I by kissing or otherwise touching another person's cold sore. Infection can also result from using utensils, cups, towels, or other objects that have been contaminated by contact with a cold sore. *Avoid touching the sore and then touching your eye; this can cause a serious infection that untreated can lead to loss of sight in the eye.*

Once infected, certain stimuli can initiate blister formation, including stress, bright sunlight, or other infections.

Incidence: Cold sores are very common. Once you become infected with viruses from the herpes family, they stay with you for life. The viruses apparently reside in nerve cells, remaining dormant until something causes them to form lesions. Stress, food allergies, sun exposure, fever, and the start of a menstrual period often act as triggers.

Noticeable symptoms: Cold sores almost always develop on or near the lips, though they can form inside the mouth or even in the nostrils or on eyelids. The first symptom is a painful tingling. Within several days one or more blisters appear. They are round, reddish, and filled with pus. They break and ooze, then form a yellowish crust. The blisters usually heal within a week.

If a fever or swollen lymph nodes develop, see your doctor. Also see the doctor if you have frequent outbreaks or if the sores are numerous and severe.

Treatment options: Nonprescription ointments containing benzocaine can be applied to cold sores to numb the pain. Painkillers such as aspirin also may help. A doctor may prescribe acyclovir ointment to prevent the viruses from reproducing. Applying acyclovir ointment or taking the oral form at the first sign of tingling may stop blisters from forming or at least reduce their severity. If bright sun is a trigger, a sunblock on the lips when at the beach or skiing can help.

Phone doctor

Colic

(KOL-ihk)

SYMPTOM

See also
Cramp
Gallstones
Infants and disease
Kidney and bladder stones
Lead poisoning
Menstrual pain

Colic in common speech refers to an attack of abdominal pain in infants. However, physicians may use the term in conjunction with other conditions that produce abdominal pain. For example, *biliary colic* is pain caused by a gallstone stuck in the bile duct. Women who suffer abdominal pain during their periods have *menstrual colic,* commonly called cramps. *Lead colic* is a symptom of lead poisoning, once common among painters working with lead-based paint and at one time caused by drinking beverages produced in stills or cider presses that were constructed with lead linings. *Renal colic* is caused by a kidney stone, either in the kidney or the duct leading from it, the ureter.

Parts affected: Infant colic is caused by spasmodic contractions of a baby's intestines. The condition occurs in one out of five babies, usually during the infant's first three or four months.

Cause: Doctors are not sure why some babies get colic. Possible explanations include an immature digestive system, overfeeding or too fast feeding, swallowing of air during feeding, allergy to milk, or even the baby's awareness of parental anxiety.

Related symptoms: Infants with colic usually turn red-faced and cry loudly, often pulling their knees up to the chest, clenching fists, and scowling. Usually the attacks come at about the same time each day and may continue for hours.

Relief of symptoms: Other than easing parents' anxiety by eliminating more dangerous disorders as the cause of colic attacks, doctors can do little to improve the situation of infant colic. Babies usually remain healthy despite bouts of colic. Often physicians suggest changing an infant's diet in some way, but this may be more important in letting parents feel that they are trying to help than in actually eliminating the symptom. Taking steps to keep the baby calm or quietly entertained and making sure that the infant is not hungry can sometimes help. Colic usually clears up by itself by the baby's fourth month.

Colitis
(kuh-LIY-tuhs)

DISEASE

TYPE: AUTOIMMUNE;
GENETIC

Phone doctor

People who experience abdominal pain accompanied by bloody diarrhea may have colitis, an inflammation of the colon or of the entire large intestine. This disease is potentially very serious.

Cause: Colitis usually refers to *ulcerative colitis,* the cause of which is uncertain—there is a genetic component, and it also is classed as an autoimmune disease. Ulcerative colitis is marked by lesions (sores, also called *ulcers*) of the mucous membrane that lines the large intestine.

Noticeable symptoms: Colitis is typically accompanied by high fever, sharp pains in the lower abdomen, and frequent diarrhea. Stools smell foul and often contain blood, mucus, and pus, or may be tarry from internal bleeding. Sometimes the stools seem to consist mainly of bloody water. Weight loss, fatigue, and joint pain may occur. ***Because the disease can develop rapidly and become life-threatening, see a doctor as soon as possible.***

Diagnosis: An instrument called a *colonoscope* will be inserted into the large intestine to examine its walls. A tissue sample may be taken and examined under a microscope to rule out cancer. X-rays may be taken.

On the Internet
NATIONAL DIGESTIVE DISEASES
INFORMATION CLEARINGHOUSE
digestive.niddk.nih.gov/
ddiseases/pubs/colitis

Treatment options: Small meals and high liquid intake along with sources of electrolytes (such as bananas—high in potassium) often help reduce symptoms. The basic medical treatment consists of antibiotics and anti-inflammatory drugs to control the disease and to prevent new flareups. Suppression of the immune system has been tried in difficult cases.

Acute attacks may require hospitalization. In severe cases surgery to remove the colon is employed; this halts the disease, but requires changes in lifestyle that many find difficult to accept.

Stages and progress: Often the first attack of colitis is the worst. Thereafter a pattern of flareups alternating with periods of remission may develop. Other parts of the body may become involved. For example, joints—especially those of the wrists, knees, and ankles—may become inflamed, and the flow of bile from the liver may be obstructed. People who have ulcerative colitis for ten years or longer have an increased risk of developing cancer of the colon.

Colon and rectal cancers

DISEASE

TYPE: CANCER

Colon cancer and rectal cancer are diseases of the large intestine. They also are called *colorectal* (кон-luh-**REHK**-tuhl) *cancer.* Many cases begin as small growths, called polyps, that eventually become cancerous. Medical procedures can detect and remove polyps in their precancerous stage. If colon or rectal cancers are detected and treated in their early stages, they are highly curable.

Parts affected: Colon or rectal cancers develop in the large intestine, which is the final portion of the digestive tract. The main part of the large intestine is called the *colon.* It opens into a short section called the *rectum,* which leads to the *anus.*

Cause: Several factors appear to increase a person's chances of developing colon or rectal cancers. These include a family history of polyps, colorectal cancers, or other cancers. A personal history of polyps or other cancers also may indicate a greater likelihood of colorectal cancer. Inflammatory bowel diseases, such as colitis and Crohn's disease, may develop into colon or rectal cancer. Diet may be a contributory cause; people whose diets are low in fiber, fruits, and vegetables

On the Internet
NATIONAL CANCER INSTITUTE
www.cancer.gov/cancertopics/
types/colon-and-rectal

Phone doctor

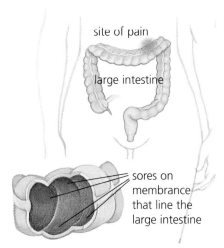

site of pain

large intestine

sores on membrance that line the large intestine

Colonoscopy
Examination of the inner walls of the large intestine is conducted with a lighted tube inserted through the anus, usually in a hospital or well-equipped specialist's office. The same instrument is often equipped with a device that can remove a small portion of diseased walls for further testing.

appear to have an increased susceptibility to colon or rectal cancers. Physical inactivity, use of tobacco, and exposure to certain chemicals, including asbestos, have also been linked to the disease. A few people have genetic diseases that tend to produce colorectal cancers; the same genes make other forms of cancer more likely as well.

Incidence: Each year approximately 150,000 Americans are diagnosed with colon or rectal cancers. An estimated 57,000 Americans and 4,500 Canadians die from these diseases, accounting for about 10% of annual cancer deaths.

Noticeable symptoms: Often there are no early symptoms, so frequent testing is necessary in older persons (see Prevention and possible actions below). A change in bowel habits that lasts more than a few days, bleeding from the rectum, blood in the stool, and cramps or constant abdominal pain may indicate the presence of a tumor. *If you experience any of these symptoms, see a doctor as soon as possible.*

Diagnosis: The physician will feel the abdomen and lymph nodes for signs of a mass or swelling. Blood and urine samples will be taken and checked for chemical abnormalities. A sigmoidoscopy or colonoscopy will be performed. In these procedures the inner walls of the large intestine are examined with a lighted tube inserted through the anus. Tissue is removed from polyps and other abnormal growths and examined under a microscope to determine if it is cancerous.

Stages and progress: Determining the stage of a cancer enables a physician to choose the most effective treatment. Staging describes the size of the tumor and whether it has spread to other organs. A widely used system assigns a stage of I, II, III, or IV. I is an early stage, with no indication that the cancer has spread beyond the colon or rectum. IV is the most advanced stage, with the cancer having spread, or *metastasized,* to distant parts of the body. Cancers caught early can nearly always be cured.

Treatment options: Surgery to remove the tumor is the most common treatment for colorectal cancers. It is seldom necessary to remove large portions of the colon. Chemotherapy and radiation may also be used if the cancer has grown through the outer wall of the intestine or spread to the lymph nodes.

Experimental vaccines given to patients in early stages of colon cancer show promise. Patients with early-stage cancers who received the vaccines improved their chances of remaining cancer-free. Some of the vaccines are synthetic; others are custom-made from a patient's own cancer cells.

Prevention: A diet high in dairy products, fruits, and vegetables appears to reduce the risk of colon or rectal cancers. Vitamin D supplements and omega-3 fats, such as fish oil, are also thought to reduce risk. High-fiber foods and statins, once thought to aid in prevention, are no longer considered helpful.

Early detection is key to the successful treatment of colon or rectal cancers. Adults age 50 and older who are at average risk are advised to have a fecal occult blood test, which looks for traces of blood in feces, every year. Those over 50 should also have a sigmoidoscopy every five years or a colonoscopy every ten years. People at increased risk, perhaps because of a family history of colon or rectal cancers, generally are advised to begin screening at an earlier age and to be tested more frequently.

Coma
(KOH-muh)

SYMPTOM

See also
Asphyxia
Bedsores
Brain
Concussion
Diabetes mellitus, type 1
Drug abuse
Embolism
Epilepsy
Head injuries
Inflammation
Poisoning
Shock

Coma is unconsciousness from which, unlike sleep, one cannot be aroused.

Part affected: The brain requires a great deal of oxygen to function, and loss of oxygen supply from any region, or from clogging of the arteries or shock, can result in coma. When coma lasts for a long time, inactivity can result in muscle atrophy (wasting away and loss of power) or in bedsores (ulcers caused by lying in the same position for long periods of time).

Related symptoms: The individual lacks any movement of the eyes and does not awake in response to sound or touch or shaking. There is even no response to pain.

Associations: Coma is a common result of various types of damage to the brain. These include physical injury from falls or blows or from the pressure of a brain tumor, aneurysm, or blood clot.

Poisoning, including drug and alcohol overdose, can also induce coma. A particularly potent combination includes alcohol taken in conjunction with other drugs. Some bacterial or viral illnesses attack the brain, causing inflammation that leads to coma.

Type 1 diabetes can induce coma, commonly called *diabetic coma* or *ketosis* (kee-TOH-suhs), by altering blood chemistry so that the blood becomes, in effect, a brain poison.

Electrolyte imbalance, which is most often caused by excessive sweating, can also cause coma. (Electrolytes, which are important cell messengers, are the sodium and potassium in the blood.)

Prevention: In many cases coma stems from risky behavior that results in physical damage or overdoses of drugs. A person with diabetes needs to monitor blood sugar, control diet, and use insulin as needed to avoid ketosis. Maintaining fluids in the body when working hard in hot weather is important as well.

Relief of symptoms: There is no treatment that is known to relieve coma unless the underlying cause is eliminated, such as relieving pressure on the brain or restoring balance to the blood supply.

Common cold

DISEASE

TYPE: INFECTIOUS (VIRAL)

See also
Allergies
Coughs
Fever
Hay fever
Influenza
Nose and throat conditions
Pneumonia
"Strep"
Viruses and disease

The common cold is a contagious and generally mild infection that causes inflammation of the mucous membranes lining the nose and throat. The resulting stuffy, runny nose and the occasional cough and sore throat that accompany the cold are the short-lived consequences of this inflammation. For these symptoms there is no cure except patience.

Cause: The common cold, also known as a *head cold,* is not one disease but a group of related syndromes brought on by any one of more than 200 different viruses. Of these the rhino (Greek for "nose") and corona (so named for their characteristic crownlike shape) viruses account for about half of all colds; six or more other types of virus are thought to cause the remainder.

Transmission: In order to infect an individual, a cold virus must gain entry to the mucous membranes that line the upper respiratory system. This transmission of viruses most often occurs via the hands, the infectious material passing from an infected individual directly to a healthy person via a handshake, for example; it may also travel indirectly via a hard surface that two individuals have touched—a doorknob, a telephone receiver, or a bathroom drinking glass.

When the uninfected person rubs his or her nose or eyes and touches the inside of the nose or the inner corners of the eyes, the virus finds its way to the membrane. There the virus is able to attach to and invade the underlying cells to cause infection. Uncovered sneezes that can project tiny virus-laden droplets into the air are a less frequent mode of travel for cold viruses.

Incidence: Young children, because they play in very close contact with each other and have not yet learned to practice simple routines for avoiding infections, are especially vulnerable to infection, with six to ten colds per year being the usual pattern. These same children then become the principal means of infecting their parents. As people age and experience cold after cold, however, they gradually develop a degree of immunity to scores of cold viruses. Young adults, for example, may have only two or three colds per year. But there are so many different viruses, and the level of immunity developed is so low, that almost no one ever gets to a point of total resistance.

Noticeable symptoms: While all colds share certain basic symptoms, these vary somewhat in severity according to the particular virus contracted. Classic symptoms—most of which arise as the result of the body trying to rid itself of the infection—include runny nose, cough, sore throat, sneezing, watery eyes, and hoarseness.

The common cold may easily be confused with other diseases. Should a high fever accompanied by overall body pain occur, the infection is more likely to be influenza, a more serious respiratory virus. An illness that includes difficulty in breathing and a persistent fever may be pneumonia, which requires medical attention. A very sore throat may be a streptococcal infection, which requires antibiotics.

Often what seems to be a cold at first will be limited to a runny nose, sneezing, and watery eyes; if it is not winter, and if the symptoms seem to come and go, the problem may be an allergy, especially hay fever, and not a cold at all.

Relief of symptoms: Medical science has no cure as yet for the common cold, and recommended treatments are designed to reduce symptoms only. If your throat feels dry, add moisture to the air with a vaporizer or humidifier. Drink lots of liquids; if there is pain, take acetaminophen at bedtime to aid sleep. Over-the-counter cold remedies may give a measure of relief to some, but they are typically combination remedies that contain more different medications than a particular cold may need. The extra substances may cause drowsiness or other unpleasant side effects. Antihistamines will suppress hay fever symptoms but have little or no effect on cold symptoms.

A physician should be consulted only if symptoms persist for more than a week or so, or suddenly worsen. In such instances a secondary bacterial infection may have developed for which treatment may be helpful or perhaps even necessary.

Prevention: Many people believe there are ways of preventing colds—by taking large quantities of vitamin C, by staying out of cold drafts, and by avoiding getting chilled or wet for prolonged periods, for example. Numerous experiments have been run in which volunteers submitted to weeks of misery to test these theories. But the only precaution that has been shown scientifically to work is frequent hand washing and keeping hands away from nose and eyes.

Wash hands

Although we think of colds as starting with a chill or draft, the virus that causes the disease is most commonly passed from person to person by touching or sneezing or by touching surfaces, such as playing cards, that have previously been touched or sneezed on by a person carrying the disease. Frequent hand washing is the best way to reduce the risk of catching the common cold.

Concussion

(kon-KUSH-uhn)

DISEASE

TYPE: INJURY

See also
Amnesia
Brain
Coma
Dizziness
Head injuries
Shaken baby syndrome

On the Internet
MAYO CLINIC
www.mayoclinic.com/health/
concussion/DS00320

An accidental fall or a sharp blow to the head can cause a concussion, a minor injury that involves no permanent damage to the brain. A concussion can occur with or without a brief loss of consciousness.

Injuries involving the head are always potentially serious. Seek medical assistance whenever you feel dazed or after loss of consciousness because of a blow to the head.

Cause: The skull provides protection for the brain, absorbing most of the shock from minor bumps and moderate blows. But sometimes impact is so intense that the brain actually moves within its protective case. Severe shaking can also bounce the brain off the inside of the skull, especially in young children. The temporary loss of function of part of the brain from such a blow is called concussion.

Concussion can make the victim feel dazed or even lose consciousness. The brain is not permanently damaged, however. Apart from some minor discomfort most people recover completely from a concussion.

More serious types of head injury arise when the blow is hard enough to cause internal bleeding or to fracture the skull. The effects of internal bleeding may not show up at first, which is why all head injuries require attention by a physician.

Incidence: About 1.8 million concussions are reported in the United States annually, but physicians believe that many people who experience concussion are not treated or examined.

Noticeable symptoms: Dizziness or loss of consciousness is possible after being hit in the head. External cuts and bruises may be minor, though external injury cannot be used to determine whether more serious internal head injuries are present. Headache for a day or two and trouble concentrating are also possible. Vision may be somewhat blurred. Faintness and nausea are common, and even vomiting.

Loss of memory also may accompany a concussion. Usually incidents occurring just before and during the accident causing the concussion are forgotten. Sometimes, though, the temporary amnesia blocks out memories of a few weeks or more leading up to the accident. The memories do return in time, with the more distant ones usually coming back first.

Phone doctor

Avoid aspirin

Remember that symptoms of more serious head injuries may not appear until hours or days after an accident. Because more serious head injury is always a possibility, *see your doctor right away when you are hit hard enough to become dazed or lose consciousness.*

Diagnosis: The doctor will look for outward symptoms of serious head injury, including dilation of a pupil in the eye, persistent confusion, difficulty in speaking, drowsiness, or an increasing feeling of tiredness. If further tests seem warranted, the doctor may order x-rays or a CT scan to be sure that the skull is not fractured or that there is no internal bleeding.

Treatment options: While recovering from a concussion, avoid any vigorous movement that may jar the head. Also, put off doing anything that requires mental concentration. *Do not take aspirin after receiving a blow to the head, however. Aspirin may contribute to bleeding.*

Stages and progress: In most instances of mild concussion there is full recovery within a few days. But for about one-third of those who suffer concussions, certain symptoms may persist, including prolonged bouts with headache and dizziness. These patients may also experience irritability, inability to concentrate, restlessness, insomnia, moodiness, or even depression.

Even up to a month after a head injury the following symptoms are a signal to return to the physician: persistent drowsiness; difficulties in speech; paralysis of any part of the body; falling or other loss of coordination; noticeable personality changes or confusion; widening of the pupil in one eye more than the other; continued loss of memory; severe headache.

Congenital digestive system conditions

Defects or illnesses that are present at birth are called *congenital*. The congenital disorders of the digestive system discussed in this entry all require immediate treatment, usually surgery, to prevent severe damage or death.

Fortunately, congenital digestive defects are uncommon. In general their cause is unknown. Most are considered to be accidents in the development process. Sometimes the defects occur in combination with other malformations, such as con-

On the Internet
KIDS HEALTH
kidshealth.org/parent/general/
body_basics/digestive.html

genital heart defects. Some are associated with chromosomal abnormalities, such as Down syndrome.

Congenital digestive system defects can be revealed by ultrasound examination or other tests during pregnancy. Such advance notice makes it possible to prepare for surgery or other treatment after birth or sometimes even before birth.

Gastrointestinal defects: The gastrointestinal (GI) tract is basically one long tube, extending from the mouth at one end to the anus at the other. During development, a blockage may occur at one or more points in the GI tract, interfering with the digestion of food and disposal of wastes. A partial blockage is called *stenosis* (steh-NOH-sihs), which means "narrowing". A state of complete closing down of the passage is called *atresia* (uh-TREE-zhuh). Atresia may in turn be either a blockage within the tube or the complete absence of part of it.

Typical locations for stenosis or atresia include:

■ the pylorus (piy-LAWR-uhs), a ring of muscle at the exit from the stomach; *pyloric stenosis* occurs in about 1 in 150 newborn boys and 1 in 750 newborn girls; two or three weeks after birth, the baby begins to vomit forcefully soon after feeding. Pyloric stenosis can be confirmed with ultrasound or x-rays. When found, it is nearly always successfully corrected surgically.

■ the small or large intestine: *intestinal atresia* (which occurs in about 1 in 2,000 newborns), in addition to vomiting and bloating, results in total lack of bowel movement.

■ the anus, or exit from the digestive system; *imperforate anus* occurs in 1 in 5,000 births, preventing bowel movements and sometimes requiring extensive surgery to remedy.

Such obstructions do not harm the fetus before birth, when nourishment comes entirely from the mother and the GI tract has very little function. But problems soon appear when the newborn begins to feed. Stenosis may seriously impair passage of food through the GI tract, and atresia halts it altogether. Without prompt surgery for either condition, starvation, dehydration, or infection may quickly lead to death.

Abdominal wall defects: The *abdomen* (AAB-duh-muhn) is the part of the body between the bottom of the rib cage and the top of the hipbone. Abdominal (aab-DOM-uh-nuhl) wall defects are abnormal openings in the front wall of the abdomen that allow some of the intestines and other internal organs to protrude.

There are two forms of abdominal wall defects: *omphalocele* (OM-fuh-loh-seel) and *gastroschisis* (gaas-TROS-kih-sihs). An omphalocele forms at the navel, or *omphalos*. In gastroschisis, the opening is located to one side of the navel. Gastroschisis, which is generally less serious, occurs in 1 of 2,700 births and omphalocele in 1 of 4,800. There is considerable variation. Only a small amount of intestine may protrude, or most of the intestines plus other internal organs may be displaced. Surgery right after birth can prevent infection and ensure the proper function of the affected organs.

Biliary atresia: Bile is produced in the liver. It then flows through bile ducts into the small intestine for disposal. Excess bile is stored in the gallbladder, from which a second duct brings the bile to join the duct from the liver. Occasionally, around the time of birth, the ducts become blocked. The bile cannot flow to the intestine and backs up in the liver. This rare condition, called *biliary atresia,* occurs in about 1 in 15,000 newborns.

The first sign of blockage is usually jaundice, as wastes build up in the blood. The bile pigment in the blood produces a yellowish discoloration of the skin and eyes. Progressive destruction and scarring, or cirrhosis, of the liver soon follow.

The causes of biliary atresia are not known, but the condition may result from an infection around the time of birth. It can also be caused by cystic fibrosis, which can plug the ducts with thickened mucus.

The first line of treatment is surgery to remove or replace the diseased ducts and to reconnect the liver to the intestine. If this procedure fails, the only alternative is a liver transplant.

Congenital diaphragmatic hernia: The diaphragm is a sheet of muscle that separates the abdomen and the chest. Its chief function is to serve as a kind of bellows that causes the lungs to expand and contract in breathing. But another function is to keep the abdominal organs, such as the stomach and intestines, from getting in the way of the heart and lungs. Occasionally, during early pregnancy, the diaphragm fails to form completely in the fetus, leaving a hole between the abdomen and chest through which some of the digestive organs protrude. This condition is known as a *diaphragmatic hernia.*

Such a hernia causes no problems before birth. But when the newborn tries to breathe, the displaced organs may not leave enough room for the lungs to expand properly. In the most serious instances, the hernia is so large that the lungs are not able to develop to full size.

A newborn with a severe diaphragmatic hernia is likely to need immediate assistance with breathing by means of a ventilator or mechanical heart-lung bypass (a procedure called *extracorporeal membrane oxygenation,* or ECMO). Once the baby is stabilized, the opening through the diaphragm is surgically repaired, either by sewing it shut or by covering it with a synthetic patch.

After surgery babies whose lungs were only displaced usually recover with little further intervention. Those with underdeveloped lungs remain at high risk and are likely to need continued assistance with breathing until the lungs have had time to grow to normal size.

Congenital diaphragmatic hernia, which occurs in 1 of 3,400 births, once was a leading cause of infant death. It remains a very serious condition but progress in treatment has greatly reduced the risk of death or lasting disability.

Hirschsprung's disease: Sometimes the nerves that control part of the large intestine fail to form, a condition called Hirschsprung's disease, or *clonic aganglionosis* (ay-GAANG-glee-uh-NOH-sihs). Without normal control the muscles of that part of the intestine cannot carry out the rhythmical peristaltic contractions that move digested wastes along. Instead the muscles go into spasm, blocking the passage of wastes from the body and causing the intestine above the blockage to swell. Because of the pattern of nerve development for the intestines, this condition, which occurs in about 1 in 5,000 newborns, most frequently affects the rectum.

The first signs of the disease, as of other gastrointestinal obstructions, do not appear until after birth. Constipation may cause the baby to become dangerously dehydrated. The walls of the large intestine normally reabsorb most of the water from food, but when the intestine is blocked, no additional water can reach the large intestine to be reabsorbed. Furthermore, bacteria in the stationary wastes may produce a violent infection called *toxic enterocolitis*. Immediate surgery is needed to remove the paralyzed segment of the colon.

Congenital heart defects

REFERENCE

TYPE: DEVELOPMENTAL;
ENVIRONMENTAL;
GENETIC

See also
Arrhythmias
Cardiac muscle
Chromosomal abnormalities
Circulatory system
Down syndrome
Endocarditis
Epilepsy
Fetal alcohol syndrome
Heart
Heart failure
Heart murmur
Patent ductus arteriosus
Rubella ("German" measles)

On the Internet
AMERICAN HEART ASSOCIATION
www.americanheart.org/
presenter.jhtml?identifier=4565

Congenital heart defects (CHD) are among the most common of all birth defects. The defects are called *congenital* because they are present at birth.

All congenital heart defects interfere in some way with normal blood circulation and cause a shortage of oxygen (*hypoxia*) in the body. Some defects are so mild they are never noticed, while others are so severe they result in early death.

Cause: While the causes of most congenital heart defects are unknown, some are produced by prenatal exposure to anti-epilepsy drugs, alcohol, or virus diseases such as rubella ("German measles"). Others are associated with chromosomal abnormalities such as Down syndrome. Most, though, occur unpredictably at an early stage of prenatal development, when the heart and blood vessels are formed.

Incidence: Congenital heart defects occur in 1 in every 100 to 150 births. About 1 million people alive today in the United States have CHDs that have been successfully treated or that are too mild to need treatment.

Common types: At least 35 congenital heart defects are known, but most are rare. The following are among the most common.

Septal defects: The most common of all CHDs are known familiarly as "holes in the heart." They are actually holes in the central walls, or *septa,* that normally separate the chambers of the right side of the heart from those of the left. They can occur between the *atria,* which are the heart's upper chambers, or between the lower chambers, called *ventricles,* or both. The holes may be so small that they cause no symptoms or heal by themselves. But large ones seriously interfere with circulation and may cause early death if not repaired.

A normal heart. Right and left are as on a person, not as seen. Red indicates oxygen-rich blood, blue, oxygen-poor blood. Arrows indicate direction of blood flow.

BELOW: Seven common defects. Purple is mixed blood.

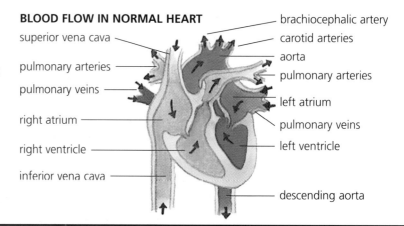

BLOOD FLOW IN NORMAL HEART

- superior vena cava
- pulmonary arteries
- pulmonary veins
- right atrium
- right ventricle
- inferior vena cava
- brachiocephalic artery
- carotid arteries
- aorta
- pulmonary arteries
- left atrium
- pulmonary veins
- left ventricle
- descending aorta

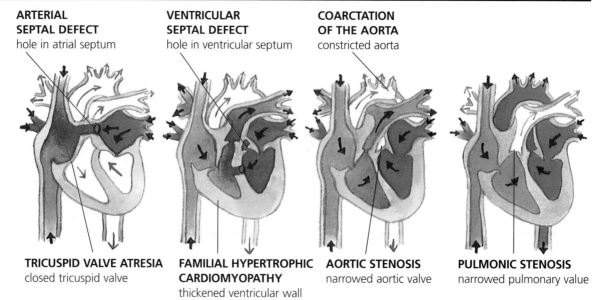

ARTERIAL SEPTAL DEFECT
hole in atrial septum

VENTRICULAR SEPTAL DEFECT
hole in ventricular septum

COARCTATION OF THE AORTA
constricted aorta

TRICUSPID VALVE ATRESIA
closed tricuspid valve

FAMILIAL HYPERTROPHIC CARDIOMYOPATHY
thickened ventricular wall

AORTIC STENOSIS
narrowed aortic valve

PULMONIC STENOSIS
narrowed pulmonary value

Pulmonary stenosis (steh-NOH-sihs, literally "narrowing"): The pulmonary artery carries blood from the heart to the lungs to pick up fresh oxygen. It has a pulmonary valve that allows blood to enter the artery but prevents it from flowing back into the heart. Pulmonary stenosis restricts the flow at or near the valve. If it is severe, not enough blood reaches the lungs, and not enough oxygen is absorbed to meet the body's needs. In such cases surgery may eventually be needed.

Aortic stenosis: The aorta is the artery that carries oxygen-enriched blood from the heart to the rest of the body. At the point where it leaves the heart is the *aortic valve*, which allows blood to flow out of the heart but not back into it. Aortic stenosis is a narrowing of the valve itself or of the aorta near it. In severe instances it may reduce the blood flow enough to cause debilitating hypoxia; it may also cause the heart to be damaged from overwork.

Coarctation of the aorta: Coarctation (KOH-ahrk-TAY-shuhn) of the aorta is a constriction of the aorta just past the point where branches lead to the upper part of the body. The blood pressure rises dangerously in these upper vessels, including those that serve the heart muscle itself, but drops in the lower ones. This is a serious defect that almost always requires surgery.

Tetralogy of Fallot (teht-RAHL-uh-jee uv fah-LOH): This is a combination of four different heart defects:

- *ventricular septal defect* (see above)
- *pulmonary stenosis* (see above)
- *overriding of the aorta,* in which the opening of the aorta is displaced to the right, over the ventricular septal defect, so that blood from both ventricles flows into it
- *hypertrophied right ventricle,* in which the right ventricle is overworked and becomes thickened, enlarged, and in danger of failure.

This combination of defects seriously interferes with circulation and usually must be repaired as soon as the child can tolerate surgery.

Tricuspid valve atresia: The tricuspid valve allows the one-way flow of blood from the right atrium to the right ventricle. Sometimes it fails to form properly during prenatal development, so that circulation to the lungs is completely blocked. The defect is quickly fatal after birth unless it is accompanied by septal defects. These allow the left side of the heart to supply blood to both the lungs and the rest of the body. The child can then live until surgery is performed.

Transposition of the great vessels: In this very serious malformation the aorta and pulmonary artery switch places. As a result, the normal cycle of blood circulation to the lungs and then to the rest of the body is broken. Oxygen-rich blood from the lungs is pumped right back to them, while "used" blood from the body is also pumped back directly, without any fresh oxygen.

Like tricuspid valve atresia, this defect is quickly fatal

unless it is accompanied by other defects. These may allow a combined circulation to the lungs and body that can keep the child alive until surgery is performed.

Noticeable symptoms: Hypoxia may cause breathlessness, weakness, fatigue, chest pain (angina), and dizziness or faintness, especially during or after exertion. Serious defects may produce *cyanosis* (siy-uh-NOH-sihs), a bluish cast of the skin caused by dark, oxygen-starved blood flowing through the body. Infants suffering from cyanosis are familiarly known as "blue babies."

Diagnosis: The presence of a heart defect may be suggested by a faint pulse or a heart murmur heard through a stethoscope. Some defects can be diagnosed from an electrocardiogram (ECG). But the most definitive evidence comes from a sophisticated form of ultrasound technology known as *echocardiography*, which can be used on infants and can also identify many heart defects prenatally, before the infant is born.

Treatment options: Some defects require surgical treatment immediately following birth while others can be treated later in life. Corrective surgery may even be done before birth. Artificial valves, pacemakers, or heart transplants may be necessary.

Prognosis depends on the type and extent of the defect but the outlook has improved dramatically in recent decades and many children with CHD can enjoy normal or near-normal lives.

Congestion

SYMPTOM

The term "congestion" is used in medicine to mean a blockage of the lungs or nasal passages that prevents air from flowing to and from the lungs. Sometimes congestion results from a swelling that blocks the passages. More often congestion is caused by a buildup or thickening of mucus—a fluid produced by glands that line the passages.

Parts affected: Congestion most often affects the nasal passages or the bronchial passages that carry air into the lungs. The lungs themselves may also fill with fluid. Sinus cavities (open spaces in the skull that are connected to the nasal passages) that become congested may cause *sinus headaches*, which cause pain in the front of the head and face.

Phone doctor

Related symptoms: Congestion of the nose or lungs interferes with breathing. Coughing frequently occurs in an effort to keep the passages to the lungs clear. Often the underlying cause of congestion is an infectious disease.

Sinus congestion may cause the head to feel stuffy, especially when combined with nasal congestion. When pressure within the sinuses increases, a severe headache may occur.

Associations: The primary causes of congestion are allergies or asthma, bronchitis, and infectious diseases of the respiratory system, especially the common cold and pneumonia of all types. More rarely congestion is the result of nasal administration of drugs such as cocaine or is a complication of syphilis.

Prevention and possible actions: Prevention depends on the cause of the congestion. Allergies and asthma can be treated before congestion develops, for example, but avoiding infection is the best way to prevent colds. Unless congestion of the upper throat blocks breathing completely, there is little serious threat to health; ***but lungs filling with fluid require treatment by a physician.*** Medicines called *decongestants* suppress the production of mucus, the fluid that is filling parts of the respiratory system or the sinus cavities.

Conjunctivitis

See **Pink eye**

Constipation

SYMPTOM

Phone doctor

Physicians usually define constipation as fewer than three bowel movements a week, but normal bowel habits vary greatly from person to person. Usually constipation is nothing more than a minor problem, but it can be a symptom of something more serious. ***If constipation persists for more than three days, or if you have blood in your stool, see your doctor.***

Cause: Constipation often is the result of diet or lifestyle. People who do not drink enough fluids or eat enough fruits, vegetables, and whole-grain foods tend to become constipated from time to time. Physical inactivity, perhaps as the result of an illness that leaves one bedridden, can also contribute to constipation.

On the Internet
NATIONAL DIGESTIVE DISEASES
INFORMATION CLEARINGHOUSE
digestive.niddk.nih.gov/
ddiseases/pubs/constipation/

Frequent use of laxatives can bring on constipation. Laxatives may clear out the bowel too completely and lead to bowel inactivity. That prompts the taking of another laxative, which again overempties the bowel and may start a cycle of frequent laxative use.

The large intestine removes water from wastes before they are expelled through the anus. The more time that wastes linger in the large intestine, the more water is removed. Therefore an attack of constipation results in dry stools that are difficult to pass.

People who have hemorrhoids may become constipated because they fear the pain that can accompany defecation during a hemorrhoid flareup. Fear of pain can also be a factor for patients with an anal fissure—a small tear in the anus.

Constipation is a common problem among pregnant women. By the fourth month of pregnancy, a woman's uterus has expanded enough to put pressure on the intestines and to increase the likelihood of constipation.

Children become constipated in several different situations. Infants on an all-milk diet after normal weaning time may develop hard stools because milk contains no fiber. Adding cereal or fruit to the diet usually helps.

Any disruption of normal bowel routine—while traveling, for instance—could result in constipation. Stress may also cause this problem.

Sometimes constipation is a side effect of prescription medications or drug abuse. Opiates, such as codeine, morphine, and heroin, prevent normal action of the bowels. A few people suffer alternating bouts of constipation and diarrhea, a condition due to irritable bowel syndrome.

Related symptoms: When constipated, you will find yourself regularly straining to make your bowels move. There is often a feeling of fullness in the abdomen and perhaps abdominal pains. A headache, nausea, and loss of appetite can accompany constipation as well. As a result of these feelings people sometimes reduce activities; this only tends to make the underlying constipation worse.

Associations: While constipation is usually a minor problem, it can be a side effect of more serious medical conditions. For example, people who have suffered a *stroke* or *paralysis* may have problems with constipation. Or someone suffering from severe depression may become constipated because he or she is eating less and not getting much physical exercise.

Constipation sometimes signals a condition called *hypothyroidism,* in which the thyroid is not producing enough of the hormone thyroxin. Other symptoms of this disorder include unexplained weight gain, sluggishness, more than usual sensitivity to cold, and dry skin or hair. ***Seek prompt medical attention for this potentially serious condition.***

Abdominal pain centered on the lower left side of the abdomen could be a sign of *diverticulitis.*

Especially for people over the age of 40, a sudden, unexplained onset of constipation might also be a warning sign of colon cancer. Your doctor will order tests if cancer is suspected.

Prevention and possible actions: Eat high-fiber foods such as fruits, vegetables, and whole-grain bread to provide the bulk needed to ensure proper bowel action. Dried fruits, such as prunes, raisins, and figs, can be especially helpful in preventing constipation. In addition, drink plenty of fluids each day and get regular exercise.

It is desirable to establish a routine and have a bowel movement about the same time each day. In any event, never ignore the urge to defecate because you are too busy.

Drink water

High fiber

Exercise

Convulsion

SYMPTOM

A convulsion is a sudden and uncontrolled episode in which many or all of the skeletal muscles contract; it is often accompanied by unconsciousness. The same symptom is also called a *seizure* or a *fit.* Often the word is used in the plural, as in "the child went into convulsions." By any name a convulsion is a striking event that may occur as a symptom of many different diseases or underlying conditions. Although it appears frightening to the observer, the symptom is not by itself necessarily dangerous.

Parts affected: The convulsion may simply affect an arm or a leg, although often it seems as if all the muscles in the body suddenly contract.

Phone doctor

Medic alert

On the Internet
MEDLINE PLUS
www.nlm.nih.gov/medlineplus/
ency/article/000021.htm

Related symptoms: Often people injure themselves accidentally while the convulsion is in process, sometimes by biting the lips or tongue or by falling or striking some object. Otherwise there is no lasting effect from the convulsion itself, although there may be further problems from the underlying disease.

Associations: About half of all convulsions occur in childhood. Convulsion often occurs in young children as a result of either a high fever or the violent coughing of pertussis (whooping cough). Children who are engaged in a tantrum can sometimes produce convulsions, perhaps by holding their breath.

In people of all ages common causes of convulsion include epilepsy, for which convulsions are often the main symptom; diabetes, in which convulsion may result from an insulin overdose; or any other condition that interferes with the proper operation of the brain, including injury or loss of blood supply. Thus convulsion can result from such serious diseases as brain tumors or abscesses, encephalitis, meningitis, head injury, heat stroke, hardening of the brain arteries, or drug or alcohol overdose. Convulsions may also occur with chronic alcoholism, cerebral palsy, some genetic diseases, and some forms of leukemia. ***Always seek immediate medical assistance for convulsions of unknown origin.*** People who have epilepsy or diabetes often carry cards identifying their condition.

Prevention and possible actions: Most people with epilepsy or with permanent or long-term brain damage—for example, from cerebral palsy or a tumor—can take regular prescription medicines that reduce or eliminate convulsions. Make sure that the person experiencing the convulsion is somewhere safe and that there are no nearby objects that could cause harm. It is often suggested that convulsions of the whole body can best be treated by putting some object, such as a rolled-up dish towel or handkerchief, in the mouth in such a way as to prevent tongue or lip biting, but this may do more damage than good. It may be helpful to loosen a buttoned-up shirt collar or a tight belt. Do not administer alcohol or splash water in the face. Call a doctor, and wait for the convulsion to subside.

Relief of symptoms: Diabetic convulsions from insulin can be warded off with any sweet food or with fruit juice; but if a physician is present, he or she can inject glucose for immediate relief. Do not try to give food to someone who is unconscious.

COPD
(chronic obstructive pulmonary disease)

DISEASE

TYPE: MECHANICAL

See also
Asthma
Bronchitis
Emphysema
Lungs
Respiratory system

On the Internet
AMERICAN LUNG ASSOCIATION
www.lungusa.org/site/
pp.asp?c=dvLUK9O0E&b=35020

COPD is a chronic, slowly progressive disease of the lungs characterized by difficulty in exhaling. It encompasses one or both of two conditions: chronic bronchitis and emphysema. The disease is permanent, and there is no cure.

Parts affected: COPD results from damage to the respiratory system over a period of many years. Chronic bronchitis may cause the airways that lead from the throat to the lungs to narrow and become clogged with mucus. This prevents air from reaching the lungs. Emphysema damages and destroys the *alveoli*. These are the thin-walled cavities in the lungs where the exchange of oxygen to and carbon dioxide from the blood takes place.

Cause: Smoking is the predominant cause of COPD, responsible for 75% of deaths from the disease in developed countries. An inherited deficiency of the enzyme alpha-1-protease inhibitor is another risk factor, and it is critical that people with this deficiency never smoke. Other factors that increase chances of developing COPD include a history of frequent childhood lung infections and long-term exposure to environmental pollutants, including dusts and ozone.

Incidence: Because COPD develops slowly, it primarily afflicts people age 50 and older. It is more common in persons of European descent, which suggests that genetic factors increase risk. It also is more common in men than women, but as the number of women who smoke has increased so has women's incidence of COPD. It is the fourth leading cause of death in the United States, accounting for approximately 125,000 deaths annually.

Noticeable symptoms: The main symptom of COPD is shortness of breath accompanied by coughing or wheezing. COPD is a "silent disease": Much damage to the respiratory system may already have occurred before symptoms become noticeable. Once symptoms appear, they may progress rapidly and become incapacitating. Walking, dressing, and other daily activities may cause extreme shortness of breath.

Diagnosis: A patient will be asked to inhale as deeply as possible, then exhale as rapidly and completely as possible. The physician will time the length of exhalation and listen for wheezing and other noises. Blood tests and other studies are used to indicate the stage of the disease.

Treatment options: Although COPD cannot be cured, its progression and severity can be controlled. Smokers will be advised to stop smoking immediately. Exercise programs to strengthen muscles will be prescribed. Lifestyle changes may be recommended to reduce stress on the respiratory system. For instance, patients may be advised to live on one floor and to avoid being around persons who smoke. Medication will be prescribed to control coughing, mucus production, and other symptoms. Supplemental oxygen and mechanical breathing assistance may be required in advanced cases. Lung transplants are an option if severe emphysema is the primary manifestation of COPD.

Prevention and possible actions: The most important way to avoid COPD is to avoid smoking. People who continue to smoke should limit exposure to pollution, including occupational hazards such as dusts and chemical fumes.

Don't smoke

Coronary thrombosis   *See* **Heart attack**

Coughs

A cough is a noisy expulsion of air that occurs as the result of irritation of the throat, trachea, or bronchial tubes. Its function is to clear these airways of the substance causing the irritation—particles of dust or smoke, incorrectly swallowed food, substances such as alcohol or pepper, or the thick mucus called phlegm that is produced by the body itself.

Most coughs are of no lasting significance, but coughs that persist for more than a few days may indicate more serious underlying factors.

Mechanism: Sometimes a cough results from a voluntary decision to expel air—for example, to attract attention—but most coughs are involuntary. Sensitive tissue lining the breathing passages signals irritation to the cough center in the brain. This triggers an automatic sequence of events:

- The brain signals the chest and abdominal muscles to tighten, and simultaneously orders the glottis, a narrow opening at the top of the larynx, to close.
- This combination of squeezing of muscles and closing of the "stopper" causes air pressure to build up in the lungs until it reaches explosive strength.
- The glottis is forced open, and the trapped air explodes outward at speeds as fast as 75 to 100 miles per hour.

Materials that travel on that air may go many feet before they come to rest unless the individual covers his or her mouth with a hand or a tissue. Such dispersion is particularly significant when the cough is transporting an infectious agent.

An involuntary cough may be either *productive* or *nonproductive*. The productive type of cough brings up, or produces, mucus or other materials. A nonproductive cough—also known as a dry cough—is one that does not expel anything but air. While the common cold may cause a productive cough, the cough that often comes with influenza is nonproductive.

When a cough results from an infection in the throat, a nonproductive cough can cause more harm than good. A more serious secondary infection such as bronchitis or pneumonia can follow if irritants are not dispatched in due time by a productive cough. The germs causing the disease can find their way to the lungs.

Associations: Various diseases that once occurred commonly in childhood have cough as one of their symptoms. The childhood viral diseases collectively known as croup are named for the characteristic barklike cough. As is the case for croup, pertussis (whooping cough) is characterized by a distinctive pattern and sound. Other diseases, including measles, may include coughing as a symptom.

Life-threatening diseases that have cough among other

Phone doctor

symptoms include pneumonias of all kinds and tuberculosis (measles may also be life-threatening). Coughs that produce blood are markers of potentially serious conditions and should be investigated by a physician.

Another relatively common type of cough is that which occurs among heavy smokers or former smokers. That cough may become so familiar a part of the individual's life as to go unnoticed. It is usually the result of chronic high levels of abnormally thick mucus in the lower bronchial airways caused by the constant presence of irritants in cigarettes and other tobacco products. The smokers' cough may be a forerunner of other more serious conditions beginning with bronchitis and escalating to emphysema and lung and throat cancers.

Relief of symptoms: For coughs due to a cold or other minor nose-and-throat illnesses, the best treatment may be drinking lots of fluids, using a room air humidifier, and sleeping with the head slightly elevated.

Two basic kinds of medications are used to treat coughs: suppressants, also called antitussives, and expectorants. Both are available in over-the-counter and prescription formulations. Side effects are rare but do occur, as do undesirable interactions with other medications. Before taking any medication, tell your doctor or pharmacist what other medications you are taking. Also alert them to other health conditions you may have, particularly problems such as heart disease, high blood pressure, diabetes, or thyroid disease.

The goal of a cough suppresant is to silence a nonproductive cough through either narcotic or nonnarcotic agents that lull the brain's cough center to be less responsive to signals of irritation. Anything that suppresses a cough should be used only for a day or two, according to package instructions, since coughs are a necessary function of the body

The most effective narcotic substance for cough relief, sold in strength only by prescription, is codeine, a derivative of opium. Because codeine is potentially addictive, has many side effects, and can interact with other medical conditions in even tiny concentrations, even over-the-counter medications containing codeine should not be taken without consulting

A cough propels germs into the atmosphere where they can travel many feet before landing on a surface or another person. Since many germs can live on surfaces for a long time and still be infectious, the person coughing can lower the risk of his disease spreading by covering his mouth with a tissue each time he coughs.

your physician. Somewhat less powerful but much safer is the synthetic cough suppressant dextromethorphan.

The goal of expectorant medications is to thin the mucus in the air passages. This loosens the mucus and makes it easier to be coughed up, thereby clearing the air passages. The compound guaifenesin is commonly used in expectorants.

Cowpox

See **Animal diseases and humans**

Cramp

SYMPTOM

See also
Circulatory system
Cryptosporidiosis
Diabetes mellitus, type 1
Diabetes mellitus, type 2
Diet and health
Fatigue
Gastroenteritis
Leg cramps
Menstrual pain
Muscles
Parkinson's disease
Peripheral artery disease
Skeletal muscles
Smooth muscles
Spinal cord
Stomachache
Whipworm

Cramp is a spasm and involuntary contraction of a muscle. Although cramps can be quite painful, they are usually harmless.

Parts affected: Any skeletal muscle may become cramped from strenuous or repetitive exertion. Cramps in the feet, legs, abdomen, arms, and hands are all fairly common. People who do not exercise often enough or who abruptly increase the amount they exercise may experience a skeletal muscle cramp during or even some time after a workout. The possible activities that cause cramp are diverse, ranging from jogging (leg cramp) to writing by hand (writer's cramp). Abdominal cramps are generally caused by contractions in the smooth muscles, such as the uterus (menstrual pain) or the stomach and intestines (indigestion or gastroenteritis).

Related symptoms: Cramp caused by physical activity usually is accompanied by a sharp or aching pain and a slight bulging of the affected muscle. Abdominal cramps caused by gastroenteritis may be accompanied by nausea, diarrhea, and fever.

Heat cramp is a skeletal muscle contraction caused by sweating. With heat cramp the patient may also have a weak pulse and dilated pupils.

Causes and associations: Heat cramp is brought on by loss of salt through sweating.

Nighttime cramping in legs and feet while lying in bed, called *recumbency cramp,* may follow strenuous exercise earlier in the day or perhaps be a result of aging (as people age, their muscles tend to cramp more easily). Recumbency cramp may also occur in people with Parkinson's disease, diabetes, and spinal cord lesions and in those receiving dialysis and some types of chemotherapy.

Leg cramp or pain that occurs while walking short distances, and that quickly goes away when walking stops, is known as *claudication,* a symptom of clogged arteries in the legs also known as *peripheral artery disease. Hypocalcemia,* a disease associated with calcium deficiency, also causes extensive muscle cramping.

Abdominal cramping may precede labor or accompany menstrual periods. Stomach or colon cancers also produce abdominal cramping, as do the parasites whipworms. But the most common cause is a viral infection of the digestive system, called gastroenteritis (sometimes known as stomach flu).

Prevention and possible actions: Drink water or other liquids before and during exercise to help prevent cramping. Stretch muscles before exercising vigorously. Gradually increase your workout instead of trying to do too much at once. In hot weather wear lightweight, loose-fitting clothing, and rest more frequently.

Relief of symptoms: Cramp usually lasts only a few minutes and often goes away by itself. Massaging the affected muscle may relieve the pain and help relax the muscle more quickly. Recumbency cramp can often be relieved by standing and walking a few steps. For heat cramp move to a shaded area, and drink water mixed with salt.

Cretinism

See **Hormone disorders**

Creutzfeldt-Jakob disease

(KROITS-fehlt YAH-kop)

DISEASE

TYPE: INFECTIOUS (PRION)

Although Creutzfeldt-Jakob disease (CJD) has historically been rare, recent developments have combined to make it better known than many more common fatal diseases. Some famous people have died from the disease, notably the choreographer George Balanchine, who succumbed in 1983. An outbreak in the 1980s occurred when some people received human growth hormone that had been infected with the disease. The epidemic of mad cow disease in Great Britain in the 1990s led to infection with a variant of CJD.

On the Internet
NATIONAL INSTITUTE
OF NEUROLOGICAL DISORDERS
AND STROKE
www.ninds.nih.gov/disorders/
cjd/cjd.htm

> **Did You Know?**
> Like many diseases, this one was named after the researchers who first identified the illness—in this case two German neurologists, Hans Gerhard Creutzfeldt and Alfons Jakob, who in the 1920s first described and diagnosed the disease.

Cause: Some cases of CJD appear to be sporadic—that is, they arise independent of any known cause in an individual. One form is thought to be genetic. Other instances arise from infection from a known source.

Transmission of CJD is similar to that of a virus, but the disease takes from 10 to 50 years to develop. Contamination of the human growth hormone probably occurred at least 8 and perhaps as many as 20 years before disease symptoms were observed in the mid-1980s. Therefore the causative agent of CJD was originally labeled a "slow" virus. But in 1985 neurologist Stanley B. Prusiner proposed that "slow viruses" are a form of protein and not viruses at all. He christened the aberrant protein form a prion (PREE-on). The prion is an altered form of a normal protein found in the brain. It has the unusual ability of transmitting its altered form to the normal protein, resulting in all of the normal protein of that type gradually changing into prions.

Incidence: CJD is rare, with one person in every million diagnosed worldwide each year, about 6,000 cases annually. In the United States the number developing the disease is about 200 each year. The symptoms appear mostly in people between 55 and 80. Men and women are affected about equally.

Noticeable symptoms: CJD begins with the mental confusion and forgetting called dementia, somewhat as in the more familiar syndrome Alzheimer's disease. Progression once symptoms appear is much faster, however, and the dementia is combined with effects on the muscles, including loss of muscle mass (known as "wasting") and movement of various parts of the body without conscious control. There may be an unusually stiff gait, difficulty in speech, hallucinations, and loss of memory as well.

Diagnosis: In addition to specific tests for dementia or muscle changes, computerized tomography (CT) brain scans can be used to determine that the brain tissue is becoming defective. Other tests, such as a spinal tap, are used to rule out possible other causes of symptoms. In later stages an electroencephalogram reveals patterns in brain waves that are specific to the disease and that confirm diagnosis. A biopsy can sometimes reveal characteristic signs in the brain, which can be confirmed after death by a brain autopsy.

Treatment options: There is no known treatment, although medications can help control such symptoms as aggressiveness or loss of muscle control.

Stages and progress: In the classic form of CJD symptoms begin to appear in middle age; young people do not get this disease in part because the infection grows so slowly. After symptoms begin, the progression is rapid, with notable degeneration from week to week. Death usually occurs within six months, although sometimes the victim may live for one or two years.

Prevention: Extra sterilization or destruction of instruments used to treat or diagnose persons with known CJD is needed to prevent transmission. Today, human growth hormone is manufactured by genetic engineering, so it cannot become contaminated. Careful screening is used to eliminate other possible sources of transmission, such as transplants.

Crohn's disease

DISEASE

TYPE: AUTOIMMUNE; GENETIC

A chronic inflammation of the intestines, Crohn's disease causes intermittent bouts of diarrhea, abdominal cramps, and low-grade fever. Attacks can be largely controlled with medical treatment, but the disease itself cannot be cured. Eventually, serious complications can develop; over half of those with the disease will need to have corrective surgery.

Cause: Medical experts do not know exactly what causes Crohn's disease, but there is a greater chance of developing the disease when a family history exists. An estimated 20 to 25% of people with the disease have a relative with either Crohn's disease or ulcerative colitis. Many share a mutation of the gene *Nod2* on chromosome 16 that increases the chance of developing the disease from two to thirty times.

Recurring inflammation in a part or parts of the intestine is characteristic of the disease. The inflammation is probably induced by an abnormal response by the immune system. The

On the Internet

NATIONAL DIGESTIVE DISEASES
INFORMATION CLEARINGHOUSE
digestive.niddk.nih.gov/ddiseases/
pubs/crohns/

protein produced by *Nod2,* for example, attacks harmful bacteria, but appears to attack benign microorganisms as well when the gene has a Crohn's mutation. The immune system may also attack the lining of the intestine.

Incidence: Formerly considered to be rare, Crohn's disease is becoming more common. In developed nations, including the United States and Canada, from 1 to 3 persons in 1,000 develop the disease. Incidence is higher among certain ethnic groups; a New Zealand study, for example, found incidence to be high in white populations and low in black and Polynesian races. Lifestyle factors, including diet, are believed to be a likely cause of increasing incidence.

Noticeable symptoms: Periodic bouts of cramping in the lower right section of the abdomen (mimicking appendicitis), diarrhea, bloody or black tarlike stools, nausea, a low-grade fever, and a general feeling of ill health or weakness are characteristic symptoms of Crohn's disease. Abdominal swelling and tenderness may also occur. Mouth lesions are common, and about a third of patients develop anal abscesses. Symptoms appear during teenage or young-adult years in most cases—90% of all patients develop the disease by age 40.

Diagnosis: When Crohn's disease is suspected, a medical history of the patient's family is taken to determine whether other family members have similar symptoms. If so, there is a greater chance that the patient has Crohn's disease rather than another inflammatory disorder of the intestines.

Other symptoms that appear only in more advanced cases of Crohn's disease may help doctors make a diagnosis. For example, x-rays may show development of abscesses and small tubelike passages leading from the small intestine to the colon, stomach, or other locations. The inside of the small intestine may also become narrower because scar tissue has formed after repeated bouts of inflammation.

Treatment options: No cure for Crohn's disease exists, but medical treatment can ease the effects of the recurring attacks. Medications reduce symptoms of Crohn's disease. Antidiarrheal and antispasmodic drugs usually reduce the patient's diarrhea and abdominal cramps. Corticosteroids have proven effective for reducing inflammation in active flareups; they may also be used in smaller doses over the long term to prevent new attacks. But long-term use of steroids may produce serious side effects, including in the more extreme instances diabetes, cataracts, osteoporosis, and hypertension. Immune-system-suppressing drugs may also be effective against Crohn's disease.

No stress

Emotional stress appears to play a part in Crohn's disease, and treatment often includes changing the patient's daily routine to reduce stress wherever possible. Nutrition is also important. Vitamin supplements and a well-balanced diet are recommended. Unless the patient's small intestine has narrowed due to scarring, the doctor may prescribe fiber supplements as well.

Eventually, a surgeon may have to remove the affected part of the small or large intestine because repeated attacks scar the bowel and cause other medical complications.

Surgery can produce dramatic improvement, but the results are often temporary. Flareups occur in another part of the intestine in over half the patients who have surgery. Repeated surgical removal of inflamed parts of the intestine can shorten the small intestine so drastically that it is no longer able to absorb enough nourishment; after that the patient must be fed intravenously.

Stages and progress: The first attacks of Crohn's disease often appear when the patient is in his or her twenties. About a quarter of those who get the disease have only one or two attacks and never experience any further problems. But for the rest, attacks may recur at varying intervals ranging from months to several years.

In about a third of all cases there is chronic inflammation of the small intestine only, usually just the final section. Half the cases show inflammation in both the small and large intestines, usually in the end of the small intestine and upper part of the large.

About one out of every five persons with Crohn's disease develops *enteric arthritis,* pain that tends to move from one joint to another, often affecting the spine. Unlike other forms of arthritis, symptoms often vanish after a few months.

INDEX

The first digit in **boldface** is the volume number; page numbers follow the colon.
Page numbers in **boldface** indicate entries.

A

Hepatitis A and E **4:84–86**
Hepatitis B **4:86–89, 8:15, 8:92**
Hepatitis C **4:89–91**
Hepatitis D **4:86–87**
Hepatitis E **4:84–86**
Herbal medicine **1:37**
Hereditary disorders. *See*
  Genetic diseases; *specific
  diseases*
Hernias **4:92–95**
  congenital diaphragmatic
  2:99–100, 3:37
Herniated disk. *See* Slipped or
  ruptured disk
Heroin **3:59**
Herpes, genital. *See* Genital
  herpes
Herpes simplex **2:87, 4:35,
  5:31**
Herpesviruses **8:102**
Herpes zoster. *See* Shingles
HGE. *See* Ehrlichiosis
Hiatal hernia **3:37, 4:40,
  4:92–95**
Hiatus hernia. *See* Hiatal hernia
Hib. *See Hemophilus influenzae*
  type B
Hiccups **3:37, 8:54**
High-density lipoprotein
  (HDL) **2:68**
High blood pressure. *See*
  Hypertension
Hip **2:28–29**
Hippocrates of Cos **2:15, 5:47**
Hirschsprung's disease
  2:100–101
Histamine(s) **1:28, 4:61, 5:11,
  6:92**
Histoplasmosis **4:22**
HIV and AIDS **4:40, 4:95–98,
  7:14, 8:14, 8:15**
  entry through birth canal
  1:109
  HIV testing **4:97**
  and immune system **5:3–4**
  as modern pandemic **3:98**
  opportunistic diseases **6:40**
  Pneumocystis carinii **4:97,
  6:105–6**
HIV infection **4:39–40, 7:15,
  8:16**
  See also HIV and AIDS
  (acquired
  immunodeficiency
  syndrome)
Hives **1:30, 4:98–99**
HLA. *See* Human lymphocytic
  antigen
Hobo spider **8:1–2**

Hodgkin's disease **4:99–100,
  5:73, 5:75, 6:93**
Hodgkin, Thomas **4:100**
Holter monitor **1:68, 1:83**
Homeopathy **1:37**
Honeybee **8:18**
Hookworm **4:100–101, 6:73**
Hordeolum. *See* Styes and
  chalazions
Hormonal system **4:101–3**
Hormone disorders **4:103–5**
Hormones **3:88, 4:101–3,
  5:102–103**
  adrenal **1:16**
  main human **4:102–3**
  and puberty **7:25–26**
  and reproduction **3:89**
Hornet **8:18**
Housemaid's knee **2:28–29**
HSV. *See* Herpes simplex
Human Genome Project **4:38**
Human granulocytic
  ehrlichiosis. *See*
  Ehrlichiosis (HGE)
Human growth hormone. *See*
  Growth hormone
Human lymphocytic antigen
  (HLA) **1:89**
Human monocytic ehrlichiosis
  (HME) **3:72**
Huntingtin **4:106**
Huntington, George **4:106**
Huntington's disease **4:31,
  4:33, 4:106–8**
  dementia **3:19–20**
HUS. *See* Hemolytic uremic
  syndrome
Hydatidiform mole **6:101**
Hydramnios **7:12**
Hydrocephalus **4:108–9, 8:4**
Hydrocortisone **3:70**
Hydrops fetalis **7:11**
Hyperactivity **1:13–15**
Hyperemesis **7:7**
Hyperopia **3:111**
Hyperparathyroidism **6:74**
Hyperplasia **4:114**
Hypertension **4:74, 4:110–12**
  and pregnancy **7:5**
Hyperthyroidism **4:47, 4:104,
  8:52**
Hypertrophic cardiomyopathy
  (HCM) **2:41, 4:113–14**
Hypertrophied right ventricle
  2:103
Hypertrophy **4:114–15, 6:4,
  7:93**
  prostate **7:19**
Hypnosis **1:36, 5:100**

Hypnotherapy **1:37**
Hypocalcemia **2:114, 5:49**
Hypoglycemia **4:105,
  4:115–16, 6:61**
Hypoparathyroidism **6:74**
Hypopituitarism **4:105, 6:99**
Hypotension **4:116–17**
  neurally mediated
  hypotension **2:71**
Hypothalamus **2:14–15, 4:77,
  6:98**
Hypothermia **4:118**
Hypothyroidism **2:107,
  4:104–5, 8:52**
Hypoxia **1:71, 2:60, 2:104,
  6:88, 7:85**
Hysterectomy **2:55, 3:91**
Hysterical paralysis **6:64**

I

IBS. *See* Irritable bowel
  syndrome
Ichthyosis **7:100**
ICU (intensive care unit) **6:31**
Idiopathic diseases **5:10**
  pain **6:57**
Idiopathic thrombocytopenic
  purpura **1:90**
Ileum **7:108**
Ileus. *See* Bowel obstruction
Imaging **3:36**
Immune deficiency **1:12–13,
  7:70**
Immune system **2:83, 5:1–4**
  ADA deficiency **1:12–13**
  and allergies **1:28, 1:30**
  autoimmune diseases
  1:87–90
  and HIV **4:95**
  and inflammation **5:11**
  rejection of prostheses **7:21**
  response to transplants **6:41**
  response to viruses **8:103**
  SCID **5:3, 6:93, 7:70–71**
  and skin **7:97**
  spleen **8:8–9**
  vaccination **8:91**
  and yeast infection **2:37**
Immunization. *See* Vaccination
  and disease
Imperforate hymen **1:41**
Impetigo **7:34, 7:101**
Implant, dental **3:24**
Impotence. *See* Erectile
  dysfunction
Incisions **8:115**
Incompetent cervix **7:12**
Incontinence **3:104, 5:5–6**

Indigestion **8:20, 8:22**
Indirect inguinal hernia **4:93**
Infantile paralysis. *See*
  Poliomyelitis ("polio")
Infants and disease **5:6–10**
  asphyxia in **1:73, 2:61–62**
  blindness from maternal
  gonorrhea **4:50**
  botulism **2:10**
  breathing difficulties in
  newborns **2:60–62**
  burping **6:16**
  colic **2:88–89**
  croup **3:2–3**
  diaper rash **2:37, 7:33**
  intussusception **5:19–20**
  pertussis **6:87–88**
  rashes **7:33**
  shaken baby syndrome
  7:78–79
  SIDS **7:88–89**
Infancy **4:53**
Infection, avoiding **1:2**
Infectious disease **5:8–9**
Infertility, spontaneous **1:90**
Inflammation **5:10–12**
  in Crohn's disease **2:116–17**
Influenza **1:54, 2:94, 3:97–98,
  5:12–13, 8:102**
  See also Avian influenza
Ingrown toenails **5:14**
Inguinal hernia **4:92–93**
Inhalant **3:58**
Inhaler **1:76**
Insects
  bites **5:25**
  and disease **8:74**
  parasitic **6:70**
  stings **5:25, 8:18–19**
  See also Mosquito
Insomnia **5:15–17**
  fatal familial **7:16**
Insulin **1:54, 3:31–32, 3:33–34,
  4:102, 4:116, 6:61**
  genetically engineered **4:34**
Insulin-resistance syndrome
  3:33
Intellectually disabled. *See*
  Developmental disability
Intelligence test **3:28**
Interferons **3:116, 4:90, 6:92**
Intermittent claudication
  5:49–50
Interstitial fibrosis **5:17–18**
Interstitial lung disease. *See*
  Interstitial fibrosis
Interstitial pneumonia **6:107**
Intraocular implant **2:47–48**
Intussusception **5:19–20**

Our thanks to the following organizations and persons who
made the photographs used in this set possible:

  Christ Episcopal Church Youth Program (Mary Millan)
  Maryknoll Lay Missioners (Jean Walsh)
  Mount Vernon Teen Task Force (Chris Webb)
  Putnam Family Support and Advocacy, Inc. (Pam Forde)

Photography assistant: Tania Gandy-Collins

MODELS
Roland Benson, Diana Brenner, Sally Bunch, Deirdre Burke,
Kevin Chapin, Michael Clarke, Michelle Collins, Bryan Duggan,
Germaine Elvy, Eugene Ehrlich, Caitlin Faughnan, Irmgard
Kallenbach, Max Lipson, Lydia McCarthy, Amanda Moradel,
Joshua Moradel, Veronica Moradel, Kate Peckham, Sara
Pettinger, Micaela Rich, Mario Salinas, Heather Scogna,
Halima Simmons, Wendy Sinclair, Barbara Totten, T.J.
Trancynger, Rolando Walker, Jean Walsh, Hannah Walsh-
Regotti, Maria Walsh-Regotti, Deborah Whelan, Gregory
Whelan, Francis Wick, Elaine Young, Leanne Young